Equity Compensation *for* Limited Liability Companies

THIRD EDITION

Casey August • Samuel P. Bryant • Amy Pocino Kelly
Wells Miller • Alan Nadel • Erin Randolph-Williams • Corey Rosen

The National Center for Employee Ownership
Oakland, California

This publication is designed to provide accurate and authoritative information in regard to the subject matter covered. It is sold with the understanding that the publisher is not engaged in rendering legal, accounting, or other professional service. If legal advice or other expert assistance is required, the services of a competent professional person should be sought.

Legal, accounting, and other rules affecting business often change. Before making decisions based on the information you find here or in any publication from any publisher, you should ascertain what changes might have occurred and what changes might be forthcoming. The NCEO's website (including the members-only area) and newsletter for members provide regular updates on these changes. If you have any questions or concerns about a particular issue, check with your professional advisor or, if you are an NCEO member, call or email us.

Equity Compensation for Limited Liability Companies, 3rd Ed.
Casey August, Samuel P. Bryant, Amy Pocino Kelly, Wells Miller, Alan Nadel, Erin Randolph-Williams, and Corey Rosen

Book design by Scott S. Rodrick

Copyright © 2009, 2019 by The National Center for Employee Ownership. All rights reserved. Printed in the United States of America. No part of this book may be reproduced or transmitted in any form or by any means, electronic or mechanical, including photocopying, recording, or by any information storage and retrieval system, without prior written permission from the publisher.

First edition, 2009. Second edition, 2013. Third edition, 2019.

The National Center for Employee Ownership
1629 Telegraph Ave., Suite 200
Oakland, CA 94612
(510) 208-1300
(510) 272-9510 (fax)
Website: www.nceo.org

ISBN: 978-1-938220-69-2

Contents

Preface v
Corey Rosen

1. A Primer on Limited Liability Companies 1
   Corey Rosen

2. Designing an Equity Incentive Plan 9
   Corey Rosen

3. Equity Compensation in Limited Liability Companies 29
   Casey August, Amy Pocino Kelly, and Erin Randolph-Williams

4. Allowing Holders of LLC Equity Interests to Be Treated As Employees 57
   Wells Miller

5. Accounting for Equity Compensation in an LLC 63
   Alan Nadel

6. A Primer on Sharing Equity with Employees in Non-LLC Companies 75
   Corey Rosen

7. Communicating with Employees About Equity 87
   Corey Rosen

8. Drafting Considerations for LLC Equity Compensation Plans 97
   Amy Pocino Kelly, Erin Randolph-Williams, and Samuel P. Bryant

   About the Authors 111

   About the NCEO 114

Preface

Corey Rosen
Founder, National Center for Employee Ownership (NCEO)

For many years, the most common advice on sharing equity with employees in a limited liability company (LLC) has been "switch to S corporation status instead." The argument was that it was too complicated to share equity in an LLC. Yet many LLC company leaders want to share equity with employees and have very good reasons for retaining their company's status as an LLC. When I asked experts in employee ownership law if it were possible to share equity in an LLC, the usual response was "yes, but it is complicated." No one seemed to want to go into too much detail about just what these complications were, however.

So, after many years of telling people that, yes, it is possible, but that we did not have any specific material or advice on the topic (because we could not find anyone who had written about it in more than the most general terms), we decided to create our own material. This book is the product of that effort. It is, we believe, the only detailed exploration of equity compensation in limited liability companies available.

The book starts with a general description of LLCs and an overview of the ways to share equity. Chapter 2 explores alternative approaches to designing plans in terms of who gets what, how much they get, when they get it, and what triggers the awards. Chapter 3 provides a detailed look at the various specific ways to share equity in an LLC. The chapter also addresses tax and regulatory issues. Chapter 4 discusses how to implement structures to allow LLC equity holders to be treated as employees. Chapter 5 describes how these plans affect a company's financial statements. Chapter 6 discusses the various kinds of equity-sharing methods available in S or C corporations. The idea here is to let readers judge whether the somewhat broader range of choices for such corporations justifies switching from LLC status. Chapter 7 explains various approaches to communicating equity compensation plans. Finally, chapter 8 discusses drafting considerations for LLC equity compensation plans.

About the Third Edition

The book was substantially revised for the third edition. The main chapter, on equity interests in LLCs (chapter 3), was replaced by a new chapter from a team of experienced attorneys. Another new chapter (chapter 4) discusses how to allow LLC equity interest holders to be treated as employees. The plan documents in previous editions have been replaced by a new chapter that discusses drafting considerations for LLC equity plans. Finally, the existing chapters on LLCs, designing equity incentives, accounting, sharing equity with employees, and communicating have been updated.

Chapter 1

A Primer on Limited Liability Companies

Corey Rosen

Limited liability companies (LLCs) have become a very popular way to organize new and smaller enterprises. The LLC is a type of legal entity allowed by state statute. There is nothing in the federal Internal Revenue Code that refers to LLCs. Instead, by default, LLCs are taxed either as sole proprietorships or partnerships, although a choice can be made to be taxed as a corporation. LLCs provide limited personal liability for the owners, flexibility in the distribution of earnings, flatter governance and management structure, and fewer paperwork requirements than S or C corporations. On the other hand, they do require that owners pay income taxes on their share of company earnings even if not distributed, often are not attractive to venture capital and private equity investors, and face differing laws in various states. Furthermore, the LLC structure is more cumbersome and a less efficient vehicle for offering equity compensation to employees than S or C corporations are.

LLC owners often say that they formed their company as an LLC because their attorney or advisor said they should. While some people clearly think through the pros and cons of different legal forms for conducting their business, others just take this advice without questioning whether an LLC really is the best choice. This book provides a basic overview of LLC issues. Because state laws for LLCs vary, and tax and other requirements can vary even more, it is important for business owners to work closely with their advisors to make sure they understand all the implications of choosing the LLC form of business. No one publication can provide the kind of detailed advice applicable to every situation.

This book is based on the assumption that your company chooses to be taxed as a partnership (if you have more than one owner) or sole proprietorship (if you have just one). If you choose to be taxed as a corporation, owners are now holding membership units that are treated like corporate stock for tax purposes, with whatever rights and benefits the membership unit is designed to have (dividend rights, voting rights, etc.). As a result, you can issue stock options or restricted stock awards, sell stock to employees, or provide phantom stock or stock appreciation rights. Our other publications such as *The Decision-Maker's Guide to Equity Compensation* provide a detailed discussion of issues involved in designing and operating these plans, so if you are being taxed as a corporation, we suggest you get that material.

What Is an LLC?

The limited liability company is a relatively new type of business form. Wyoming passed the first LLC law in 1977; the other states eventually followed suit. While the laws for LLCs are similar from one jurisdiction to another and sometimes identical, they are not all the same. Some states impose entity taxes on LLCs; a few impose some level of income tax. A few states have different governance requirements as well. If an LLC operates in more than one state, it may be subject to multiple tax and possibly governance rules.

The impetus behind the creation of LLC law was to provide a simpler and more flexible way for small businesses to organize than corporate law usually permits. It was intended that businesses would be taxed as proprietorships or partnerships while providing their owners with the limited liability available to corporate shareholders. LLCs are owned by "members" rather than shareholders. The term is roughly analogous to partners or shareholders, but with some notable differences. LLCs must have at least two members if they are to be taxed as partnerships (a one-owner LLC will be taxed as a sole proprietorship or a corporation for federal tax purposes). The members create an "operating agreement" that functions similarly to a corporation's bylaws. The agreement specifies how the LLC will be governed and managed, how profits and losses will be allocated, and what the member rights are (including voting, buy-sell arrangements, and distributions of earnings). LLC agreements can specify whether a member will be the manager or someone else will serve in that capacity.

Key Organizational Issues
Limited Liability

Like corporate shareholders, LLC members can avoid personal responsibility for losses or liabilities of the LLC beyond what the LLC can pay. This is not an unlimited right, however. Several circumstances can still "pierce the corporate veil" and give rise to personal liability, including:

- Contracts that members sign, such as personal guarantees for debt or performance
- Failure to deposit taxes withheld from employee wages
- Intentional fraud, reckless behavior, or illegal acts
- Personal and direct injury of someone or property

In some cases, the "corporate veil" may also be pierced if tax authorities can sustain the position that the LLC is really not an entity separate from a member's personal interests. Establishing one's house as an LLC to avoid personal liability for defaulting on the underlying mortgage, for instance, would not be effective protection.

Governance

Unlike a corporation, an LLC does not require a board of directors, although some kind of governing or advisory body may be advisable and may be required if there are outside investors. Instead, an LLC's members make decisions about the company subject to the operating agreement. A few states require more formal governance procedures, however, such as an annual member meeting, something normally only required of a corporation.

Allocation of Earnings

Unlike S or C corporations, LLCs need not allocate earnings pro rata to capital ownership. In an S corporation, owners receive a share of earnings based on their respective percentages of corporate ownership; in C corporations, distributions of earnings are based on specified stock rights but must be proportional to ownership within the same classes of stock. LLC members are taxed not necessarily based on their membership interest percentage, but rather based on whatever agreement the members have made for allocating earnings. This agreement may be stated in the operating agreement, may take the form of income-only partnership interests, or may be just an understanding among the LLC members.

Another difference between a corporation and an LLC is the manner and extent to which the business's earnings are allocated annually. In the case of an LLC, all of the net income of the business is allocable to the members who pay personal income tax on their respective amounts regardless of distributions they receive during the applicable year. Similarly to partners in a partnership, the LLC members may agree that a partner may be allocated a disproportionate percentage of the LLC earnings based on whatever business factors they choose.

This flexibility is one of the major advantages of an LLC. It is especially useful in the case of LLCs where one party invests capital (e.g., venture capital or private equity) and another puts in "sweat equity" (i.e., performance of services for less than full pay). In an S corporation, for instance, if a shareholder purchases 20% of the corporate stock, then he or she will be allocated 20% of the corporate net earnings. But if that same 20% shareholder purchases 20% of the stock and also puts in a year of sweat equity to build the business, he or she may not receive more than a 20% share of the corporate net income, although the parties could agree to also pay additional compensation in recognition of the shareholder's efforts. In the same situation with an LLC, however, the LLC members may simply choose to allocate a greater portion of the company's net earnings to that individual to compensate for sweat equity. Alternatively, they may agree to compensate the individual by awarding more ownership (i.e., member units) in the LLC.

The allocation-of-earnings approach must have a substantial economic effect; i.e., there must be a good business reason for doing it, other than to avoid taxation. Provided the allocation of earnings is not based on tax avoidance, the allocation generally will be respected by the IRS. Allocating more earnings to an owner with a lower tax rate and less to one with a higher rate, absent some other compelling business reason, likely would be problematic. Similarly, care should be taken with the allocation of passive income and losses in an LLC, a subject beyond the scope of this primer. This should be discussed with a tax professional prior to making any special allocations of income or loss.

Members

S corporations are permitted to have up to 100 shareholders and still retain the S corporation status. In contrast, LLCs and C corporations may have an unlimited number of members or shareholders. S corporations may have only one class of stock; LLCs and C corporations can have different rights attributed to different classes of ownership. S corporations may not be owned by certain prohibited entities, including C corporations, other S corporations, most non-taxable entities, most trusts, other LLCs, partnerships, or nonresident aliens. LLCs may be owned by anyone. LLCs are rarely used in some industries (e.g., venture capital) because the associated tax effects are inconsistent with the objectives of the owners. LLC members also may have different rights or benefits attached to their ownership besides how earnings are allocated, such as special distributions, governance, or the ability to cash out their ownership interests.

Dissolution

The LLC has a permanent life unless a time of dissolution is specified in the operating agreement. Similarly, one or more members may leave and the other members agree to continue the business. The operating agreement must be specific on this eventuality to avoid inadvertent termination.

Mergers and Other Ownership Transfers

If an LLC is merged into another company, it is not eligible for tax-free reorganization as provided by Internal Revenue Code Section 368. The LLC can first be terminated and S or C status chosen, but if the change and merger come within a close time frame, it will likely be considered a "step transaction," whereby the IRS takes the position that it is still an LLC.

LLCs can, however, be sold to other companies just like corporations, subject to the tax issues discussed below. Ownership interests can also be transferred to anyone or any entity, with some restrictions varying by state. In S corporations, by contrast, transfers can be made only to other S owners.

Taxes

A limited liability company is taxed as a sole proprietorship (if there is only one owner) or a partnership unless the LLC "checks the box" on an IRS filing to be taxed as a corporation. As a sole proprietorship or partnership, members are taxed on their pro-rata share of earnings unless the operating agreement specifies otherwise. This is the share of the actual earnings of the LLC, not the earnings that are distributed (earnings may be retained to grow the company, for instance). These earnings, in turn, are taxed at the individual member's personal tax rates. Members usually must make quarterly estimated income tax payments. While the federal government levies no tax on the LLC, some states do.

One difference between an LLC and an S corporation or C corporation is how employees are taxed. In a corporation, a shareholder-employee is considered an employee for all normal payroll and benefit purposes. When a shareholder-employee receives compensation, the employee pays half of the payroll taxes (through withholding) and the company pays the other half. Contributions to qualified benefit plans are not taxable to the employee but are deductible to the employer. In an LLC, the member pays the full amount of the payroll taxes in the form of self-employment tax. The total is currently 12.4% of pay up to the current year's Social Security wage base for the Social Security component of self-employment tax, plus 2.9% of all pay for the Medicare component. The member does not qualify for such qualified benefits as retirement or health insurance plans sponsored by the employer. Although the LLC member pays twice what an S corporation shareholder pays, they both pay the same when the S corporation's share of taxes is also considered. Because they are not employees, members must file estimated income tax returns and get K-1 statements, which add considerably to tax filing complexity. Based on a 2016 IRS ruling, any employee with a profits or capital interest, vested or not, is considered a member, not an employee, for tax purposes.

Another difference between a corporation and an LLC is the manner and extent to which the business's earnings are taxed each year. In the case of an LLC, all of the net income of the business is allocable to the members who pay personal income tax on their allocated amounts regardless of distributions they receive during the applicable year. If a member has a 40% interest in an LLC and the LLC earns a profit of $100,000 during the year, that member is allocated $40,000 of income even if he or she receives only a $20,000 distribution. On the other hand, a C corporation that earns a profit of $100,000 must pay corporate income tax on the full amount. If a distribution of that income (e.g., a dividend) is made to shareholders, they must pay income tax on those distributed amounts. Hence, the use of a C corporation usually results in double taxation of the corporate profits.

The 2017 tax law added a new wrinkle that may make it more appealing to file as an S corporation. Owners of pass-through entities can now deduct up to 20% of their net business income from their income taxes (see chapter 3 for details).

At the time of sale of LLC member units, a single capital gains tax generally is imposed on the gain (with some exceptions, e.g., receivables). This is different from a C (but not S) corporation, where an *asset* sale would trigger double taxation by virtue of a corporate capital gains tax on the appreciated value of the assets for the corporation and another capital gains tax for the shareholders on the sale of the company's shares. A *stock* sale, however, generally is not subject to double taxation, and a merger for stock in the acquirer may be tax-deferred altogether.

Conclusion

The flexibility of LLCs makes them attractive vehicles for those who wish for the flexibility of a proprietorship or partnership while retaining legal protection for the owners. Unfortunately, while they are simpler and more flexible than C or S corporations, they are considerably less so on issues concerning equity compensation for employees. In fact, some advisors suggest that companies wishing to share equity with employees should select regular corporate status because employees more readily understand stock options and restricted stock than partnership interests. We believe they may be too hasty in their recommendations, as the rest of this book will show. Equity compensation in the case of an LLC can provide for significant incentives that are performance-based. The range of choices may be narrower in the case of an LLC, and there are some remaining tax uncertainties and complexities, but effective performance-based incentives certainly can be structured in the LLC.

Chapter 2

Designing an Equity Incentive Plan

Corey Rosen

A variety of issues must be considered when designing an equity compensation plan for employees in an LLC. This chapter is not intended to provide specific guidelines on how to structure a plan but rather to raise the issues companies need to consider. In making these decisions, company leaders should consult with peers and advisors as well as evaluate available survey data on industry practices.

This chapter provides the broad outlines that should help readers decide what approach is most appropriate. The next chapter provides detailed information on the sometimes complicated tax issues that can come up with these plans. The best approach is to choose an approach that makes sense in terms of your goals, and then work with an attorney to understand the specific tax implications.

How Much to Share

The first decision is how much ownership to share. The most typical way owners of closely held companies decide how much ownership to share is by setting aside an amount of equity or equity rights that is within the maximum dilution level with which they are comfortable. This approach can create problems, however.

Typically, once this number is set, a large portion of this equity is either provided immediately to existing employees or allocated to employees over a few years. The problem with this strategy is that allocating too much too quickly leaves relatively little equity to give to new employees. In a growing company, that can lead to a severe problem in attracting

9

and retaining good people. It can also create two classes of employees, some with large equity grants and some without them. Moreover, this model often does not create an explicit link between employee effort and the rewards of ownership.

A second approach focuses on what percentage of compensation must be provided in the form of equity in order to attract, retain, and motivate people. These decisions need to be based on competitive considerations of what people could receive elsewhere as well as on discussions with employees to get a sense of how much they expect. Finding relevant information about competitive pay practices means more than simply referring to a salary survey. Competitive pay information should be based on data from companies that might compete for the same employees, rather than just the company's business competitors. Often this includes companies in other industries that may hire individuals with similar experiences and skill sets as those of the company's current employees.

Rather than thinking about "how much" in terms of a total percentage of company shares or total compensation, it might make sense to use a more dynamic model based on performance. In this approach, the issue for existing owners is not "what percentage of the company do we own?" but "how much is what we own worth?" Owners in this model would rather own 10% of an $11 million company than 90% of a $1 million company. This notion can be incorporated into an explicit plan by telling employees that if the company meets or exceeds certain targets, they will receive a percentage of the incremental value created by that performance in the form of equity or equity rights. If the company exceeds its goals, then, by definition, sharing part of the surplus value leaves both the employees and the existing owners better off than they would have been. The targets can be based on whatever performance goals are appropriate for the company, such as sales, profits, market penetration, or whatever else is critical to the company's future. Given the volatility in the economy over the last 15 years or so, the company should also include risk management considerations in the selection of relevant performance targets. Providing substantial equity grants when the company has an exceptionally good year or two may come back to haunt the company if the company's fortunes then decline for some period of time. Risk can be managed by putting caps on the total awards available under any target plan, for instance.

It is also important to consider the "internal equity" of awards. A common problem in equity plans is that employees believe they are not getting what they deserve, something they assess primarily based on what they perceive other people are receiving. Few employees would argue that everyone should be paid the same, but most would contend that everyone should receive awards consistent with their relative contributions to the company. This problem has been starkest in relationship to executive pay, but even at rank-and-file levels, it is not uncommon for companies to pay people doing very similar jobs very different amounts of equity, perhaps because of the timing of when they came to work (more awards were available or the shares were more opportunely priced) or what was perceived as necessary to hire them. Nobel Prize-winning research has shown that perceived equity in economic transactions will often trump purely "rational" economic logic. Employees will be more cynical and demotivated if they believe that their awards are inequitable relative to what top executives receive. Boards and compensation consultants may (rightly or wrongly) argue that this can benefit the entire company, but employees will be slower to accept these arguments than the CEO's peers. Fairness consistently shows up as one of the most, if not the most, important determinant of work motivation and turnover intention, so this is not a small issue.

The fairness issue often comes up in merit-based plans. While it might seem fairer and more efficient to give the lion's share of the awards to the best performers, research shows that about 70% of the workforce believes it is in the top 10% of performers. Thus, any merit-based program that loans awards to a relatively small group will create a lot of people who believe they are being treated unfairly. One way to help preserve the benefits of a merit-based approach and create more of a perception of fairness is to get employee input into what the merit criteria should be. Even if the result is a somewhat broader or perhaps less economically "optimal" result, if employees buy into the formula in advance, then the unfairness problem can be significantly eased.

How Important Is the Tax Treatment of an Equity Plan Choice?

A key driver in choosing an award structure is how important potential capital gains treatment is to employees. Capital interests and profits interests both make it possible for recipients to get capital gains treatment on the ultimate exercise or sale of their awards. Under the 2017 tax law (popularly known as the Tax Cuts and Jobs Act of 2017), the differential is meaningful for higher-income employees (income would include salary and what the awards end up being worth). It might seem that capital gains treatment is still a much to-be-desired outcome for employees, although the company cannot get a tax deduction for any income treated as a capital gain. For instance, you might read about an employee who gets a $1 million payout and only has to pay 20% in taxes at the federal level but would pay a top marginal rate of 37% as ordinary income if the award is not eligible for this treatment. But for the vast majority of companies reading this article, the amounts paid out will be much smaller. The 37% rate does not kick in until someone reaches $500,000 in taxable income (when filing singly), meaning that the differences in tax treatment are often much less dramatic.

The calculations of the effects of this depend on the filing status of the individual, and the state's treatment of capital gains. There is no easy rule of thumb on this, but, in general, it is likely only managerial or highly skilled employees, such as programmers, would see much of a difference in their taxes because for most of the workforce, the marginal income tax on the award would not be more than ordinary income tax. In addition, employees with these awards might not be eligible to be treated as employees for tax purposes, as explained below, which can be costly and complicated. Finally, awards taxed as ordinary income are deductible to the employer, but awards taxed as capital gains are not. (See chapter 4 of this book, however, for a discussion of how an LLC might be able to have holders of these interests still be treated as employees.)

If getting capital gains treatment for employees is not a key outcome, then companies should look at equity-equivalent awards, described below.

What Kind of Equity?

The kinds of equity vehicles a company chooses depend largely on the purposes of the plan. While that may seem obvious, it is far too common for companies to select an equity vehicle because "that's what other people do," or "that's what my advisor understood best," or "I didn't know there were other ways to do it." Beware of advisors whose discouragement of one kind of a plan or another may really be their way of saying, "I don't know how to do the other types."

This chapter assumes that the company is not electing to be taxed as an S corporation or setting up subsidiaries taxed that way.

Sharing equity in LLCs is more challenging than in S or C corporations. In fact, as noted in the preface to this book, advisors frequently tell clients that if they want to share equity with employees, they should switch to S corporation status, which allows them to use options, phantom stock, restricted stock, stock appreciation rights, and similar plans. S corporations are taxed similarly to LLCs, but are less flexible in terms of how earnings are distributed. While employee equity awards in LLCs present more complex tax considerations than is the case in S or C corporations, there are approaches that can be effective.

Forms of Equity Available in an LLC

There are three main forms of actual equity interests available in an LLC:

- *Capital interests:* Capital interests can be compared to restricted stock in an S or C corporation. They grant the employee the right to share in the capital value of the company through the receipt of a share of the proceeds upon sale of the company.

- *Profits interests:* A profits interest will entitle the owner both to capital appreciation and profits of the business.

- *Options:* A company can issue an option to acquire an equity interest that entitles a recipient to purchase LLC interests at a later date for a price equal to or greater than the price at grant. That can be based on a number of years or an event (such as sale of the company) or both. An option holder is generally not considered an owner for tax purposes until exercise of the award.

Any type of interest may be subject to restrictions, such as a vesting requirement. Any may be forfeited if the employee is engaged in wrongdoing at the company or goes to work for a competitor.

Equity-Equivalent Rights

Rather than directly granting the above interests, companies can grant a right to acquire them later or the right to receive the equivalent of their value. These have no formal legal name but generically are equity-equivalent rights or synthetic equity. Most commonly, these would be the LLC equivalent of what in an S or C corporation would be phantom stock or stock appreciation rights (SARs). This book refers to them as unit rights and unit appreciation rights respectively.

The company gives the employees a grant of a hypothetical number of capital interest units (unit rights) or profits interest units (unit appreciation rights). With unit rights, on vesting, the employee has the right to full value of that number of units (as with phantom stock); with unit appreciation rights, on vesting the employee has the right to the increase in the value of that number of units (as with SARs). The employee might be paid in the cash value of the units (in the case of unit rights) or their increase in value (in the case of unit appreciation rights), or alternatively the employee might receive part of the award in the form of cash sufficient to pay tax on the award, with the remainder of the award delivered in actual membership units.

Basic Tax Issues

An employee's receipt of a profits interest in exchange for services is not taxable upon grant if certain safe harbor tax requirements are satisfied, including the requirement that the interest not be sold within two years of receipt. If these requirements are not satisfied, there is some uncertainty about the income tax consequences arising from the grant of a profits interest to an employee. When the employee redeems his or her profits interest (by selling it back to the company or to a third party), the gain is taxed as either a short-term or long-term capital gain, depending upon how long the interest was held by the employee. Employees with profits interests are taxed as partners rather than as employees, so their income is reported on a Schedule K-1 and is not subject to income tax withholding.

The typical agreement stipulates that profits interest holders will receive no distributions of earnings until a liquidity event. So when that happens, the gain is all capital gain. Note that some practitioners believe that not providing such a right makes people not really partners, as is required for a profits interest to qualify, but the norm is not to provide these rights. If a company does provide a share of profits to profits interest holders, then that is taxed as ordinary income and increases the basis by that amount when the stock is sold. So if Sally has a profits interest that has $50,000 in gains at the time of the liquidity event but has received $10,000 in taxable income, she pays capital gains tax on $40,000.

If Sally does get a distribution, and thus needs to pay tax on that, then companies normally make a distribution to allow her to pay that amount. That would then reduce her basis by that amount. All of these complexities help explain why interim profits distributions are not the norm.

An employee who receives a capital interest in exchange for services recognizes compensation income in the year of the award. The amount of income that is recognized equals the fair market value of the interest at the time of grant, less anything paid by the employee for the capital interest. If the interest is subject to a substantial risk of forfeiture and is nontransferable, as is typically the case, then the recognition of ordinary income tax is delayed until the forfeiture restriction lapses, unless the employee makes a timely Section 83(b) election. If a Section 83(b) election is not made, then ordinary income tax is paid on the value of the award at the time it vests. Any additional appreciation in the value of the capital interest is subject to either long- or short-term capital gains tax, depending upon how long the capital interest is held following recognition of ordinary income. An employee can also make an 83(b) election on a profits interest, in which case the employee would be eligible for capital gains tax treatment on the sale of the resulting membership interest after exercise. If granted at fair market value, the initial grant has no current liquidation value (it has a value only if the unit price increases), so there would be no immediate tax obligation. In both cases, however, if an 83(b) election is made, the employee receives a K-1 statement requiring payment on a share of the LLC's earnings. As with profits interests, the employee is considered a partner, not an employee, for tax purposes.

If a Section 83(b) election is made but the award never vests, the employee may not claim a refund from the IRS for the ordinary income taxes that were paid. The company receives a tax deduction for any amounts on which the employee pays ordinary income tax. Under the partnership taxation rules, there is a question about whether there is also a "deemed sale" when a capital interest is awarded or forfeited, resulting in potential income tax consequences for other holders of capital interests in the company.

Granting an option to acquire an equity award is not a taxable event for either the employee or the company. The exercise of an option to acquire an equity interest will result in taxable ordinary income equal to the increase in the value of the award for the employee and a deduction for the company. Note that the tax occurs on exercise, even if the interest is not yet sold. If it is not sold, then the remaining increase in value is taxed as a capital gain. The exercise of an option on a profits interest would not be taxable for the employee or deductible for the company if the tax requirements for nonrecognition of tax on a profits interest were satisfied.

Based on a 2016 IRS ruling, employees with any capital or profits interests, vested or unvested, are treated as members, not employees, with the adverse tax effects discussed in chapter 1 of this book. Many attorneys also propose workarounds for this issue, such as choosing to be taxed as an S corporation (which would make them employees), tiered organizational structures where the recipient is the employee of one of the subsidiaries, or an employee leasing company. These are all complex issues that need to be evaluated with an attorney.

If recipients are not treated as employees, they have to file K-1 statements and, usually, estimated income taxes. Not being treated as an employee is potentially costly. LLC members paid self-employment taxes, as high as 15.3%, up to $128,400, in 2018. An employee pays only half that; the employer the rest. They do not get tax-deductible employee benefits. For employees who are not at very high income tax levels, this can mean that the benefit of getting a profits interest or capital interest that can qualify for capital gains treatment is minimal or even negative. Some lower-bracket filers pay no capital gains taxes at all. For others, given that only higher-income employees will have marginal tax rates higher than capital gains rates, companies need to work through carefully just who would ultimately benefit from this kind of treatment.

For tax purposes, unit rights and unit appreciation rights are treated in the same way as a bonus: the employee pays ordinary income tax on the receipt of the cash award, and the company is entitled to a corresponding tax deduction. The employee is treated as a regular employee for tax purposes.

Complexity Concerns

Many companies will choose one kind of award or another because it is less complex to administer, understand, and tax. This is more of an issue in an LLC, where the tax issues can be very complex and somewhat uncertain. In fact, this is why many advisors urge companies to switch to S status, where the tax issues are simpler. If employees find they have a great deal of difficulty understanding how an award works, or see the tax treatment as just too difficult to grasp relative to other kinds of pay, the value of the award can be diminished substantially. It might be better to choose a simpler alternative equity approach, such as equity-equivalent awards, even if these awards may have less favorable long-term tax consequences because they never qualify for capital gains treatment.

As with all the choices below, keep in mind that companies can give different employees different kinds or mixes of awards, with different rules being applicable to each.

Granting Existing Value or the Value of Future Increases Only

Capital interests, profits interests, or synthetic equity give the employee the existing value of the ownership plus any appreciation (much like giving an employee a share with or without dividend rights in a corporation). That means the employee reaps the benefit of the embedded value that has been previously created. This would be most logical in cases where the company has been running for a while, and the early employees have not yet received any equity awards. "Full-value" awards effectively give these employees some retroactive benefit for their work. These awards also make sense if the intention is to ensure that employees receive something even if the value of the company does not increase or increases too slowly to make the awards appealing.

In contrast, options on a capital interest or profits interest, like equity appreciation rights, provide only a share in the future growth in value. If a company is granting awards very early on when there is little existing value, these appreciation-based awards can provide significant value to employees, much like full-value awards. Down the road, however, they are very different.

One problem with appreciation-based awards is that the single most important factor in determining their value is volatility. In the formula that accountants use to assess the present value of the award of a stock option, for instance, volatility is the single most important factor. This may seem counterintuitive. Wouldn't you prefer an option on a stock that has less dramatic ups and downs? But consider that with an option, you can ignore the downs (just don't exercise the options) and take advantage of the ups. A more stable stock has lower high points (but also higher low points), providing less of this leveraging opportunity.

This has a number of additional insidious effects. First, it can encourage excessive risk-taking by top decision-makers, especially if their expected time horizon with the company is shorter than the term of the equity award. Second, it introduces a lottery effect into the incentive structure. Two employees receiving identical awards may have significantly different opportunities for gains if they were hired at different dates when the equity had a different value. Finally, appreciation-based awards can engender cynicism among employees who view equity as a lottery whose benefits may go to the lucky and to the insiders who know best when to exercise.

This may be less of an issue in an LLC than it is in other companies, especially public companies. LLC valuations tend to be done annually, absent some specific event, and may "smooth out" some of the external factors that create volatility for stocks in general. Nonetheless, LLCs can still be subject to the same problems as corporations, especially if the market for their products or services is highly variable.

Who Is Eligible and Who Will Actually Get Equity?

In the past, the answer to the question of who was eligible was very simple for most companies: just the "key" people. In some ways, this is still how companies view equity; it is just that their definition of "key" has changed. For many companies, everyone is a key person. Many LLC companies have a flat management structure and are pushing down more decision-making to all levels, asking employees to make business decisions on a regular basis. Managers at these companies reason that if they want people to think and act like owners, they should make them owners. At the same time, for some companies in some labor markets, it is necessary to provide options at all levels just to attract and retain people. For companies in these situations, the answer to "who's eligible?" is simple—everyone is.

One set of issues that some companies consider, but that they probably should not, is the so-called "1/n" or "free rider" effect, and the related "line-of-sight" problem. The argument here is that an equity award cannot be much of an incentive to an employee who cannot see (has no line of sight to) just how his or her work actually affects the value of the business. This is especially problematic in larger organizations where employees not only don't have a clear line of sight to the award but also can figure they can "free ride" on the efforts of others.

These arguments are appealing but empirically wrong. Research shows that motivation at work is much more complicated than a simple economic calculation. Few employees go to work each day thinking, "If I do x, I get y, but if I do x + a, I get y + b, so if y + b is large enough, I'll do x + a." In reality, this is really not the case. Research shows again and again that most people's efforts at work are a function of how well their job functions fit their skills, whether they have opportunities for meaningful input into decisions affecting their jobs, how much they trust management and management trusts them, whether they find the job engaging, and whether they believe what they and the company do has value.

Equity sharing becomes important in this context not so much as an incentive for behavior but as a reward. If people are asked to act like owners and are treated like owners, they will be more productive and make larger contributions in terms of new ideas and information. If they then are denied an opportunity to benefit from what they add, they will feel manipulated and back away. If, on the other hand, they feel they are equitably rewarded relative to what others contribute or that they are all part of a team sharing in the results, they are much more likely to stay committed. So the question of who gets equity should be based on which employees should be thinking and acting like owners.

Tenure

At the simplest level, companies can require that people work a minimum amount of time, often one year, before they become eligible for equity awards. This ensures that each employee has at least some commitment to the company.

Full-Time/Part-Time

In the past, it was unusual to provide equity to part-time employees. Innovators like Southwest Airlines, however, have provided options to everyone, arguing that many of their part-time people would (or if properly rewarded could) become long-term employees.

Performance or a Universal Rule?

Equity can be granted according to some kind of merit judgment; on a regular, universal schedule such as annually, or upon hiring or promotion; or it can be granted or vest upon the achievement of individual, group, or corporate objectives. These methods are not mutually exclusive; many companies use a combination of these techniques.

The core issue here is that, on the one hand, including everyone who is eligible according to some formula rules out management discretion, which employees may see as arbitrary or political. It also may help foster a team atmosphere in which everyone sees that they have a stake. On the other hand, some employees may feel cheated if they think they have been exceptional performers but receive unexceptional rewards. This suggests that some combination of the two can be appealing, provided the basis for rewarding excellence is one that most or all employees see as reasonably fair—a tricky business, but one many companies have done well at, albeit in a variety of ways. Some companies, for instance, use 360-degree performance reviews in which everyone reviews everyone else, others use very specific and transparent financial or other measurable targets, and others seek employee input in designing rating systems.

A typical merit-based approach would provide work unit managers (or a single manager in a smaller company) with a number of awards that can be granted to employees in the group based on performance appraisals. An alternative to individual merit judgments is to provide that a pool of equity awards will be given to a work team upon the achievement of the team's goals. Many companies, of course, will simply name specific individuals, usually top managers, who will receive equity, but the company will define their allocation based on merit assessments of some sort.

At the other end of the spectrum is an automatic formula based on salary levels. This can be for one employee or every employee. For instance, a number of larger companies provide all employees who meet basic service requirements with 10% of pay every year in stock options. The argument behind such formulas is that salary reflects management's judgment of an employee's contributions to the company, and equity is simply another form of compensation.

Many companies provide awards on hiring, then make additional grants periodically or upon promotion. Linking additional grants to promotion gives employees an incentive to improve their skills and rewards those people the organization believes are making greater contributions. On the other hand, an overemphasis on promotion-related grants can mean that employees who are very good performers but who are not in jobs that can easily lead to a promotion are overlooked.

Refresher grants give employees additional awards when they exercise some of the options or other equity benefits they were previously granted. For instance, if an employee has 1,000 options on a capital or profits interest and exercises 200, then the employee would be given new options on another 200 shares at exercise. The theory here is to maintain a constant level of ownership interest in the company. Similarly, refresher awards might be granted when the company issues additional equity interests so that an employee maintains the same percentage of potential ownership as was held before the dilution. While these automatic additional grants help to keep the employee's equity interest high, other owners might object to the ongoing dilution.

How Often Should Awards Be Granted?

Equity inherently involves risk, but the design of plans can accentuate that risk. Companies that provide one-time grants of appreciation-based awards and grant them only upon an event, such as hiring, promotion, or meeting some corporate target, wind up with employees whose ownership interest in the company is based on the price of stock at a single point in time. This is not a problem with full-value awards, which do not have an exercise price based on the stock's trading price on the grant date.

Granting appreciation-based awards infrequently accelerates the risk of equity both for the employee and the company because equity granted at a high price may never be "in the money"; awards granted at a low price may cost the company more than it ever intended when the awards are redeemed. Employees who happen to receive their equity awards at a good time end up doing very well, while those who receive their grants when the price is not so favorable don't do well at all. Creating an ownership culture of "we're all in this together" can be very difficult in these circumstances.

For many companies, the best way to deal with these potential problems is to provide grants in smaller amounts but more frequently or to grant full-value awards such as restricted equity or phantom equity. Frequent grants work best for companies using equity as a compensation strategy. Startups whose equity value is close to zero or that use large initial grants to attract people away from other opportunities may find this less appropriate. It also is not appropriate for companies that want simply to make occasional grants at the discretion of the company, often on the attainment of some corporate milestone. These companies see equity more as a symbolic reward than as an ongoing ownership strategy.

The periodic allocation "dollar-cost averages" the awards, smoothing bumps in volatile markets. This approach also gives employees more of a long-term, ongoing stake in the company. With the vesting schedules attached to the repeated grants of awards, employees are provided an even longer-term interest in the company's performance. Finally, there will be fewer big winners and losers among employees with otherwise similar jobs.

Frequent grants are not all good news, of course. The more often awards are granted, the more complex their administration becomes. There is much more data entry, many more forms to file and disseminate, and many more errors that can be made. It may also become complicated because of frequent tax withholding and tax reporting.

When Will Employees Be Able to Use the Awards?

There are two principal issues in deciding when employees will be able to translate their equity into cash: vesting and exercise periods. Vesting generally provides that an employee accrues an increasing right to the awards granted based on the number of years worked. However, there is a growing use of performance vesting, in which vesting is a function of company, group, or individual performance. As various targets are met, the equity awards become increasingly vested. The exercise period is the time between an award's vesting and its expiration. Some types of awards may vest automatically upon exercise, especially equity-equivalent rights. Outright grants of capital or profits interests might vest at grant, but more commonly would have a vesting period. Once vested, there typically would be no further deferral of the actual receipt of the award.

Options present a different scenario. Here the employee might become fully vested in a right to acquire a profits or capital interest, but choose to defer it until later for tax or cash flow reasons. The most common exercise period for stock options in S or C corporations is 10 years. Grants of restricted stock (stock that is tradable only after certain conditions, such as working for a defined period of time, are met) do not have an exercise period; instead, the restrictions lapse upon vesting, typically after three to five years. Given that many LLCs may have shorter time horizons than public companies (they may be working toward a sale or an initial public offering), they may want a shorter period in which an award can be exercised.

Vesting schedules are fairly consistent across companies, with three- to five-year graduated vesting the most common schedule. Sales, profit targets, and cash flow are the most common performance triggers. A few companies allow employees to exercise their awards only when a defined event occurs, such as the achievement of a certain stock price or earnings goal. This accomplishes two things. First, it provides an incentive to meet the goal, and second, it reassures investors that dilution will occur only if the company meets certain targets. Once these targets are met, employees are normally given a certain amount of time to exercise the award, anywhere from a few months to several years.

Alternatively, a company could provide that awards can be exercised only upon the occurrence of an event, such as a sale or going public.

In closely held companies, allowing exercise of an award only upon sale of the company or an IPO is a very common approach. If an option is exercised or the company allows restricted stock to vest before then, employees end up owning stock and having a tax obligation. Unless the company can provide a market for the shares (an issue discussed below), this combination may not be perceived by the employee as much of a reward. Companies and employees must evaluate just how likely these events are to occur, however. Management is often excessively optimistic about how marketable the company is.

It is also important to consider that if equity compensation awards all become exercisable upon sale or an IPO, buyers of the stock may not find the company so valuable. A growing number of closely held companies are restricting exercise to sometime after a sale or an IPO (in a sale situation, this requires the acquiring company to provide options in the new employer) to ensure that there are adequate employee incentives in place following the sale or IPO.

Providing a Market for the Shares

Providing for liquidity of equity awards is one of the most important of all design issues. Most closely held companies solve the problem by limiting the exercise or sale of equity awards to when the company is sold or goes public. This makes sense for companies that realistically see these alternatives as likely to happen in the foreseeable future. Some company leaders, however, assume that they can provide for marketability only upon these events because a closely held company, for one reason or another, cannot provide a market itself. There are, in fact, alternatives for those companies and for companies that prefer to stay closely held and have no plans to sell or become public. These companies can provide an internal market by buying back the equity interests themselves or allowing other employees to buy them. This requires proper cash flow planning. Alternatively, an LLC could convert to a C or S corporation and set up an employee stock ownership plan (ESOP), which can buy the equity (now converted into shares) with pretax dollars through an ESOP trust.

Purchasing vs. Grant

A key consideration for many employers is whether employees should pay anything for their equity. At one extreme are employers in closely held companies who see the chance to own equity as itself a valuable benefit, even if it is offered at fair market value. At the other are those who believe employees cannot or should not take the risk to invest in company equity, but do want them to have a stake in the company. Several considerations apply to any choice on this matter:

- Do employees have the resources to buy equity? If not, is the company willing to lend them the money? If the loan carries an interest rate less than fair market value, there are possible tax implications with respect to the loan.
- How many employees will buy equity, either at full value or a discount? The results are often surprising and disappointing and may not provide enough people with an equity stake to accomplish the "ownership culture" objectives the company hopes to achieve.
- Even if many employees buy equity, will the distribution of ownership be enough to create a real stake in the outcome for most people? Employees whose financial obligations (or consumer preferences) leave them with little discretionary income, as well as employees who are risk-averse, may end up with only token amounts of equity.
- If there is a discount, how much will it be? Discounts may result in taxable income to the employee.
- Where options are issued, is paying for the exercise of an option good enough? If an employee uses cash or shares to exercise an option, is that enough to satisfy the company's desire to have people buy shares, even though there is a certain gain for those who sell their shares immediately?

In most companies, widespread ownership does not occur solely through an equity purchase plan. For some companies, however, broad ownership is not the goal. Rather, the objective is to engage specific employees and/or to raise capital. There is a perception that executives will have a greater interest in the company's success if they have some "skin in the game."

Perceptions vs. Reality

In classical economics, people are "rational" economic actors by definition. That means that they make choices about things based on maximizing their economic value. For instance, if people have the choice of having $1,000 now or a guaranteed $1,200 12 months from now, as rational actors, they would wait. It turns out that in reality this is not an accurate model of how people behave. Three notable characteristics are especially important for equity awards:

- *People overvalue current rewards:* Most people in the example above take the $1,000 now. They greatly undervalue the time value of money.

- *People value upside risk less than downside risk:* Researchers have asked people if they would make a double or nothing bet if they had lost $50. Most said yes. But if they had won $50 rather than losing $50, most said they would turn down a double or nothing bet. In the stock market, this helps explain why people hold on to losing shares too long.

- *People are willing to pay for perceived fairness:* In an often repeated experiment, people are asked to accept or not accept an offer to split $10 between them and someone else. If the split is $5/$5, everyone is happy, but if it is $7 and $3 or less, most people getting the $3 will say no—even though it means neither party gets anything.

An employee equity award works much the same way. The equity award will pay off only well into the future, carries uncertainty about how or if it will be paid for (because it will have liquidity only upon a sale or IPO), has some immediate tax consequences before the recipient is able to cash it in, and is granted to employees in ways that seem inconsistent with their value. All these factors greatly diminish the value of the award in the employees' eyes. As a result, the employer must dole out more than probably it wishes to provide the incentive effect sought. So while employers often want to design awards that seem most favorable to their liquidity, that reward only very long-term employees (even though most people are not sure when they receive the award if they will stay a long time), have no clear liquidity event, and have tax consequences that the employer does not cover, this "favorable" design may be a waste of equity. Similarly, if equity awards are perceived as unfair, employees who receive what they see as the short end of the stick will feel punished, not rewarded, even though the employer is giving them something extra. The employer will be in a worse position (in terms of employee attitudes) than if they had made no grants at all. Consequently, it is imperative in plan design to remember how people actually behave, not how they "should" behave.

Conclusion

Designing an effective equity plan is a difficult balancing act. There are no perfect approaches. The financial and organizational significance of these plans demands that they be considered at least as carefully as any other major investment of company assets and time, not just picked at random or based on limited information. Try to talk to peers who have set up plans (the NCEO can help its members identify other companies with plans), interview different consultants, read enough to feel comfortable with plan structures, and seek the input of board members and, preferably, employees about what kind of plan will work best—and be prepared to make changes as you learn more.

Chapter 3

Equity Compensation in Limited Liability Companies

Casey August, Amy Pocino Kelly, and Erin Randolph-Williams[1]

A limited liability company (LLC) is an attractive organizational form for many privately held businesses. LLC formation under state law is typically simple, and LLCs, like corporations, offer their owners, referred to as "members," insulation from personal responsibility for company liabilities. Additionally, the governance of LLCs is generally simpler than under a corporation, and LLCs are eligible to be treated as partnerships (and disregarded entities) for tax purposes, whereas incorporated entities are not.

  As LLCs have become more prevalent, so too has the desire to provide equity compensation to LLC employees and other service providers in order to attract and retain valuable talent to work toward increasing the value of the company, thereby benefitting all members. Although providing a service provider with equity compensation in the LLC may result in additional administrative and tax complexities for the business and the service provider, businesses and service providers often find that the benefit from such an arrangement outweighs the associated burden. As further discussed below, the most common forms of equity and equity-like compensation in an LLC (classified as a partnership for

---

1. The authors thank Gena Yoo, a law student at University of Pennsylvania and a Morgan Lewis summer associate, for her contributions to this chapter.

tax purposes) consist of capital interests, profits interests, options, and phantom equity. Each form of equity compensation has its own set of benefits and tradeoffs that must be considered before granting to a particular service provider. In other words, in the LLC equity compensation world, one size does not fit all.

This chapter generally discusses the federal tax treatment of LLCs and associated equity compensation, as well as certain relevant securities law issues, to provide a framework for thinking about the manner in which to provide incentives for the business's management and other service providers.[2] However, this discussion is intended only as a high-level primer on the topic and does not consider all possible issues that may be relevant in a particular situation. Businesses, their principals, and their service providers should seek specific legal advice before adopting an organizational legal or tax form for their business or implementing a particular form of equity compensation.

Tax Treatment of LLCs[3]

An LLC as an organizational form is authorized under local law (i.e., state law) and is not a creature of the federal tax law. Instead, under the current tax regime established in 1997 with the release of the so-called "check-the-box" regulations,[4] an LLC can generally select its tax classification. That is, an LLC can decide whether to be classified either as a (1) corporation, or (2) depending on its number of members, either a partnership or an entity disregarded as separate from its owner (a "disregarded entity").

By default, if an LLC has more than one member, it is classified as a partnership for federal income tax purposes, and an LLC with one member is classified as a disregarded entity. Alternatively, an LLC can elect to be classified as an association subject to tax under subchapter

---

2. This discussion addresses only U.S. federal tax matters and does not address any foreign or state and local tax matters. Additionally, this discussion only considers the treatment of U.S.-based service providers and privately held businesses.
3. See Internal Revenue Service Publication 3402, *Taxation of Limited Liability Companies* (2016).
4. See Treas. Reg. § 301.7701-1 et seq.

C of the Code[5] (a C corporation) or, if the LLC satisfies certain initial and ongoing eligibility requirements, under subchapter S of the Code (an S corporation). After choosing its initial tax classification, an LLC may decide to change its classification, although post-formation changes in tax classification may be subject to certain temporal restrictions and lead to unanticipated tax results. An LLC's operating agreement, which generally sets forth the economic and administrative rights and responsibilities of LLC members, should clearly state whether the LLC is intended to be treated as a partnership or disregarded entity, or whether it will elect to be treated as a C corporation or an S corporation.

This chapter generally focuses on LLCs taxed as partnerships, but also briefly considers LLCs electing to be treated as C corporations or S corporations.

Corporations

For an LLC with a C corporation classification, the LLC will be subject to tax under the regular rules applying to corporations under subchapter C of the Code. LLC earnings will generally be subject to two levels of tax: one at the LLC entity level when earned, and one at the shareholder level for corporate distributions out of current or accumulated "earnings and profits" (generally, current or retained earnings). A member of an LLC taxed as a C corporation (a shareholder for purposes of the Code) may also be an employee of the LLC, with wages paid to such a person subject to general employment compensation and income tax treatment.

An eligible LLC may instead elect to be taxed as an S corporation. S corporation earnings are generally subject to only a single level of tax imposed at the S corporation shareholder level. S corporations, however, are subject to certain entity-level taxes, most notably for S corporations with a C corporation history or that acquired property from a C corporation in a tax-deferred transaction. As with a tax partnership (described below), the tax results of an S corporation generally "flow through" to its shareholders as reported to them on a Schedule K-1.

---

5. All references to the "Code" in this chapter are to the Internal Revenue Code of 1986, as amended, and all "Section" references are to the Code, unless otherwise specified.

S corporations are subject to a host of eligibility requirements that must be maintained at all times, which make operating as an S corporation less flexible than operating as a tax partnership. The requirements for S corporation eligibility include that (1) the entity is a domestic corporation for tax purposes; (2) there are no more than 100 owners, all of whom are either an individual (not including a nonresident alien), a decedent's estate, an estate of an individual in bankruptcy, certain trusts, certain tax-exempt organizations, or a qualifying employee stock ownership plan described in Section 4975(e)(7) (ESOP);[6] and (3) there is only one class of equity (based on economic rights, not voting rights, so that there effectively may not be preferred stock in an S corporation). Under certain circumstances, financial instruments not expressly labeled as stock may nonetheless be treated as stock for purposes of the S corporation qualification rules.

The second-class-of-stock restriction on S corporations limits the types of equity compensation that may be issued by an S corporation. However, the regulations do provide "safe harbors" for certain qualifying equity compensation arrangements to not be treated as stock for this purpose. A service provider call option safe harbor may apply to certain types of non-transferable and bona fide compensatory call options. Additionally, the regulations include a safe harbor for a deferred compensation arrangement that satisfies the following requirements: (1) it does not convey the right to vote, (2) it is an unfunded and unsecured promise to pay money or property in the future, (3) it is issued to an individual who is an employee in connection with the performance of services for the corporation (and is not excessive by reference to the services performed), and (4) it is issued pursuant to a plan with respect to which the employee is not taxed currently on income. S corporations generally attempt to comply with these safe harbors to mitigate risk to their S corporation election.

---

6. Recent non-binding IRS guidance suggests that the permission for an ESOP to be an eligible S corporation shareholder extends to an LLC that has elected to be taxed as an S corporation (PLR 201538021 [June 18, 2015]). The issues related to the establishment and maintenance of ESOPs, including S corporation sponsored ESOPs, are complex and beyond the scope of this chapter.

A significant distinction in the equity compensation context between an S corporation and a partnership is the employment status for federal tax purposes of owners working for the corporation. Unlike the case with a tax partnership (as described below), a member of an LLC taxed as an S corporation (shareholder for tax purposes) may also be considered an employee of the LLC. As long as such a person is paid "reasonable compensation" for services, additional payments from the LLC/S corporation to the owner/employee are not subject to employment tax as distributions from the LLC/S corporation in respect of the person's ownership interest. Specifically, the owner/employee does not pay Social Security and Medicare taxes on the amount of non-compensation distributions from the corporation.

When determining what is reasonable compensation, case law and Internal Revenue Service (IRS) guidance require an analysis of the facts and circumstances of the situation to determine whether the salary paid is reasonable, including the following: (1) the nature of the S corporation's business; (2) the nature of the owner/employee's duties and responsibilities; (3) the employee/owner's qualifications; (4) the time and effort the owner/employee devotes to the business; (5) dividend history; (6) aspects of compensation arrangements, such as whether there are compensation agreements, the timing and manner of paying compensation, and whether a formula is used to determine compensation; (7) what comparable businesses pay for similar services; and (8) compensation as a percentage of profits, and compensation compared with the amount of the distributions and payment to non-owner employees. Reasonable compensation issues must be kept in mind when establishing the salary of an S corporation shareholder. Reasonable compensation issues for S corporation shareholder-employees will also be relevant for determining the amount of such a person's Section 199A "pass-through deduction" discussed below.

> *Example:* Elena forms an LLC for her consulting service and elects to have it taxed as an S corporation. Elena is an employee of this LLC and receives a $50,000 salary, which is reasonable compensation based on the facts and circumstances. In addition, $100,000 of the LLC's net income flows through to Elena as reported on her Schedule K-1, and the Company distributes the $100,000 to Elena. Since the

allocation of income and distribution is not considered employee wages, neither Elena nor the S corporation likely needs to pay Social Security or Medicare tax on this amount.[7] In this situation, Elena and her corporation pay a total of $7,650 in employment taxes ($50,000 x 15.3% = $7,650; 12.4% for Social Security and 2.9% for Medicare).

Partnerships

An LLC with multiple members that has not elected to be taxed as a C corporation or S corporation is generally taxed as a partnership. A partnership tax classification enables an LLC and its members to (1) benefit from additional flexibility in structuring the LLC's business and capital structure (particularly as compared to an S corporation structure) and (2) avoid double taxation on LLC earnings. The remainder of this chapter following the discussion of disregarded entities immediately below, unless otherwise noted, assumes that an LLC is classified as a partnership for tax purposes.

A partnership is not subject to an entity-level tax for federal income tax purposes. Rather, its items of taxable gain, income, loss, deduction, and credit are directly attributed or "allocated" to its partners, and the partners are taxed on their distributive shares of the partnership's taxable items regardless of whether the partners receive distributions from the partnership. However, these taxable items are generally classified for tax purposes at the partnership level as if the partnership were a separate taxpayer, and a partnership must file an informational tax return setting forth the amount and character of its taxable items attributed to its partners. A partner's share of the taxable items of a partnership is generally based on the allocation section of the partnership's operating agreement. Such an operating agreement does not directly allocate the tax items of the partnership; the allocation section assigns items of partnership income or loss for "book-for-tax" accounting purposes. Under Section 704(b), to the extent such a book allocation relates to, or carries with it, corresponding taxable income, gain, deduction, or loss, such tax items are allocated in the same manner that the corresponding book item is allocated.

---

7. But see Code Section 1411 (3.8% so-called Medicare tax on net investment income).

In general, there are no eligibility requirements for partnerships akin to those for S corporations. Any individual or entity can own an interest in an LLC classified as a partnership, and multiple classes of ownership providing different economic rights to LLC operating and liquidation proceeds are permitted. LLCs classified as partnerships may change their classification to an S corporation or C corporation, often in a manner that does not create a taxable event for the LLC members, whereas the converse change in classification from a C corporation or S corporation to a partnership could create a significant taxable income or gain recognition event.

An LLC classified as a tax partnership generally allows for more flexibility for operating and determining the owners' relative economic rights in a business than a corporation does. However, added tax reporting and accounting complexity corresponds to the flexibility in operating as a tax partnership under the rules of subchapter K of the Code.

Disregarded Entity

An LLC that is not treated as a corporation for federal income tax purposes and that has only one member is treated as an entity disregarded as separate from its owner for income tax purposes, often referred to as a "disregarded entity." This means that the LLC's income, deductions, gains, losses, and credits are reported on the owner's income tax return, rather than being reported on any LLC income tax return.

However, a disregarded entity is considered a corporation for the purposes of (1) employment tax withholding and (2) collection of income taxes and certain excise taxes.[8] This means that the single-member owner of a disregarded entity LLC must collect and pay employment tax with regard to the entity's employees, and such owners are subject to self-employment tax on the net earnings from their self-employment related to the LLC's business activities.[9]

---

8. See Internal Revenue Service, Publication 3402, *Taxation of Limited Liability Companies* (2016).
9. See Self-Employment Tax Treatment of Partners in a Partnership That Owns a Disregarded Entity, 81 Fed. Reg. 26,693 (May 4, 2016).

New Pass-Through Deduction

Section 199A, enacted with the new tax reform legislation commonly known as the Tax Cuts and Jobs Act of 2017,[10] provides a taxpayer other than a corporation with a deduction for up to 20% of its qualified business income (QBI) from partnerships, S corporations, and sole proprietorships, as well as 20% of its aggregate qualified REIT dividends, qualified cooperative dividends, and qualified publicly traded partnership income, subject to certain limitations. The deduction is available for tax years beginning after December 31, 2017, and terminates for tax years beginning after December 31, 2025. Employment compensation, including reasonable compensation from an S corporation, and nonpartner capacity payments under Section 707 do not qualify as eligible QBI. This is a personal deduction that is not dependent on whether filers itemize. Aside from other limits noted below, this deduction cannot exceed 20% of the excess of personal taxable income minus net capital gains. The following generally discusses the Section 199A deduction as it applies to an individual's QBI.

- Single filers with less than $157,500 of taxable income and joint filers with less than $315,000 of taxable income (amounts are given as of 2018 and are subject to annual cost-of-living adjustments) are eligible for the full 20% deduction for QBI.

- For a single filer with taxable income in excess of $207,500 or a joint filer with taxable income in excess of $415,000, such an individual's otherwise eligible deduction for QBI is the lesser of (1) 20% of the QBI or (2) the greater of (a) 50% of the individual's allocable share of the business's W-2 wages or (b) the sum of 25% of the individual's allocable share of the business's W-2 wages plus 2.5% of the individual's share of the unadjusted basis (cost) of qualified property of the business (generally, depreciable business assets). However, no QBI deduction at all is allowed if the business generating the QBI is one of a number of "specified service trade or businesses." These restricted personal services businesses involve the performance of services in the fields of health, law, consulting, athletics, financial services, brokerage services, or any business whose principal asset

---

10. P.L. 115-97.

is the reputation or skill of one or more of its employees or owners, or that involves the performance of services that consist of investing and investment management, trading, or dealing in securities, partnership interests, or commodities. Engineering and architecture services are explicitly excluded from this list of restricted personal services businesses.

- Filers who fall between the $157,500/$315,000 and $207,500/$415,000 taxable income dollar limits are subject to a potential phase-out of the Section 199A deduction with respect to their QBI. For an individual whose QBI is generated by a "specified service trade or business" mentioned above (health, law, etc.), the 20% QBI deduction is subject to an income-based phase-out and also is limited to a phased-in limit based on such individual's allocable share of the business's W-2 wages and qualified property. For an individual whose QBI is not attributable to a specified service trade or business, the 20% deduction is subject only to a phased-in limit based on the individual's allocable share of the business's W-2 wages and qualified property.

Notwithstanding the current complexities and uncertainties of this new Code provision, the Section 199A pass-through deduction can provide a meaningful benefit for owners of certain pass-through tax business (i.e., non-C corporation businesses). The new pass-through deduction also may effectively increase the benefit of equity grants to employees by allowing them to now take advantage of the deduction. Again, only sole proprietors (including an owner of a disregarded entity), partners, and S corporation shareholders are eligible for the pass-through deduction.

Types of Equity Compensation for an LLC and Certain Related Federal Tax Consequences

Four primary types of equity or equity-like compensation are available in the context of LLCs classified as partnerships for tax purposes: capital interests, profits interests, options, and phantom unit and phantom unit appreciation rights plans (also referred to as phantom plans). This discussion presumes that these grants are made in exchange for services and considers certain relevant federal tax consequences of each. However, the tax rules applying to partnerships under the Code are exceedingly complicated. Accordingly, this discussion is intended only to provide a general overview of certain federal tax implications of granting equity compensation in LLCs classified as partnerships, and is not intended to provide an exhaustive discussion on the topic.[11]

Capital Interest

A capital interest is an LLC equity grant that entitles the recipient of the interest to share in the proceeds if, at the time of grant, the LLC sells all of its assets at fair market value and distributes the proceeds in a complete liquidation of the LLC.[12] That is, the recipient has a grant-date economic right in the preexisting capital of the LLC based on a grant-date sale of the company assets for fair market value and liquidation basis, as well as potentially its future profits.

Like all equity compensation, a capital interest could be granted subject to vesting conditions, so that the interest is subject to a substantial risk of forfeiture until it becomes vested, or a capital interest could be granted so that it is fully vested on the date of grant. If the capital interest is subject to vesting conditions, vesting may be based on the recipient's continuing to provide services to the LLC for a specified period of time or meeting certain performance hurdles. In practice, unvested LLC interests are generally forfeited if the recipient terminates service or commits a crime or other act of misconduct.

> *Example of a capital interest:* Amy is employed by XYZ, LLC, which holds assets with a fair market value of $200. Amy is granted a 10% interest in XYZ, LLC, which, under the entity's operating agreement, would entitle Amy to a share of 10% of the proceeds if XYZ, LLC sold all of its assets and immediately liquidated ($200 x .10 = $20). Amy's interest constitutes a capital interest.

---

11. For an in-depth discussion of the federal tax rules applying to tax partnerships, including equity compensation out of tax partnerships, see McKee, Nelson, and Whitmire, *Federal Taxation of Partnerships and Partners,* 4th ed. (Thomson Reuters/Tax & Accounting, 2007) & Supp. 2018-1.
12. Rev. Proc. 93-27, 1993-2 C.B. 343.

The tax treatment of the grant of compensatory capital interests is not certain under the law and could produce unexpected results. Accordingly, LLC businesses often choose not to grant capital interests in order to avoid the associated tax complexity and uncertainty.

Tax Consequences of Granting a Fully Vested Capital Interest

The grant of a fully vested capital interest, or a capital interest that is not subject to a substantial risk of forfeiture, is taxable to the recipient upon grant in an amount equal to the fair market value of the capital interest less any amount paid for it.[13] The grant of a fully vested capital interest is treated as compensation income to the recipient, which is taxed at ordinary income rates.

The impact of a grant of a capital interest on the LLC and the other LLC members is not certain. Because the grant of an interest in preexisting LLC capital effectively "shifts" credit for this capital (i.e., accreted untaxed value) from the existing members to the capital interest recipient, it is arguably possible that the grant could cause a taxable income or gain event for the LLC and/or preexisting members.[14] However, proposed Treasury regulations issued in 2005,[15] if finalized, would avoid this result by clarifying that Section 83 applies to the recipient, with the deemed payment treated by the LLC as a guaranteed payment for services under Section 707(c), thereby producing an LLC compensation deduction presumably allocated to the preexisting members. In other words, the LLC and the existing members would have no income or gain from the grant, but the service recipient grantee would.

Tax Consequences of Granting an Unvested Restricted Capital Interest

The tax treatment of a grant of an unvested capital interest is not certain, including with respect to the recipient. Upon grant of an unvested capital

---

13. See Section 83(a)(1); Treas. Reg. § 1.721-1(b)(1).
14. Cf. Treas. Reg. § 1.83-6(b) (providing that the payment for services with appreciated property results in the payor realizing gain as if the payor sold the property for its fair market value).
15. See Prop. Reg. §§ 1.83-6(b) (2005), 1.721-1(b)(2) (2005); Fed. Reg. Vol. 70, No. 99D, p. 29675 et seq.; Notice 2005-43, 2005-1 C.B. 1221.

interest, the recipient could have no taxable income until the rights in the capital interest vest, or are no longer subject to a substantial risk of forfeiture for purposes of Section 83.[16] Under this characterization, when the capital interest eventually vests, the value of the capital interest is treated as compensation income, less the amount paid for the interest, and the LLC and the other members are treated in the manner described above for the grant of a fully vested capital interest (subject to the same uncertainty).

Although an unvested capital interest may not be taxable upon grant, the recipient can elect to include in income the value of the interest in the year of grant under Section 83(b). This Section 83(b) election may be used by the recipient to effectively control the timing and amount of income inclusion for tax purposes.

When a Section 83(b) election is made, under the tax treatment described above, the capital interest becomes taxable at the time of grant in an amount equal to the fair market value of the interest on grant date over the amount the recipient paid for the interest. No taxable event occurs when the interest eventually vests. A timely Section 83(b) election could be advantageous because when the recipient sells the interest after it vests, appreciation in the value of the interest from the date of grant until the date of sale may be eligible to be taxed at preferential capital gains rates rather than ordinary income rates. More specifically, a Section 83(b) election allows the recipient to not take the vesting date value of the interest into account as ordinary income so that the recipient may benefit from post-grant appreciation in the value of its capital interest at capital gains rates on exit, other than for such gain or income considered attributable to the LLC's so-called "hot assets" (e.g., appreciated inventory, cash method of tax accounting accounts receivable, or depreciation recapture on fixed assets).[17] It is important to note that a Section 83(b) election must be made within 30 days following the grant. A potential negative impact of making a Section 83(b) election occurs if the recipient later ceases to provide services before the interest vests so that the interest is forfeited. In this event, the recipient cannot obtain a refund of the taxes paid upon making the Section 83(b) election, and the recipient's ability to use any tax loss associated with

---

16. See Prop. Reg. §§ 1.83-6(b) (2005), 1.721-1(b)(2) (2005).
17. See Section 751.

this forfeiture will most likely be limited. As a practical matter, recipients generally will make a Section 83(b) election when the value of the capital interest is low on the date of grant and the value is expected to increase by the vesting dates.

When a recipient makes a Section 83(b) election upon the grant of an unvested capital interest under the treatment described above, the LLC and the other members are treated in the manner described above for the grant of a fully vested capital interest (subject to the same uncertainty).

Profits Interest

A profits interest entitles the recipient only to share in the future profits and appreciation in value of an LLC following the date of grant.

> *Example of a profits interest:* Arlene is employed by ABC, LLC, a multi-member LLC classified as a partnership for tax purposes. The current fair market value of ABC, LLC's assets is $200. If Arlene is granted a profits interest at this time, all future profits and growth in the value of the LLC property above $200 could be shared by Arlene as an owner along with the other owners. For example, if Arlene is granted a 10% profits interest (as reflected in the LLC operating agreement), she may participate in 10% of all future profits and growth in value. Assume that four years later ABC, LLC, which has not generated any profits or losses in the interim period, sells all of its assets for $300 and then liquidates. At that time, Arlene would be entitled to $10 ($300 - 200 = $100; $100 x .10 = $10). If ABC, LLC generated operating profits in the interim period, Arlene could receive allocations of such profits (and receive associated distributions as set forth in the LLC operating agreement) without jeopardizing her profits interest status. Whether Arlene receives allocations of operating profits and associated distributions immediately after her grant or only at a later date (e.g., based on a valuation or cash distribution threshold or only on a liquidity event) is a generally considered by parties to be a commercial or economic matter and not a tax matter.

The profits interest has become the ubiquitous form of equity compensation to provide an incentive for LLC management and other important employees, given its more certain tax treatment and economic features (as compared to capital interests). The profits interest is also preferred to options, which are effectively the economic equivalent of a profits interest, based on the tax benefits to a profits interest recipient. As discussed below, option recipients typically do not exercise their options until an exit or liquidity event, in which case their proceeds are taxed as compensation at ordinary income rates. A profits interest, in contrast, may permit the recipient to receive exit or liquidity event proceeds taxed at preferential capital gains rate (aside from any "hot asset" gain described above). The tradeoff for this beneficial tax result is that the profits interest recipient is a member of the LLC (i.e., a partner in a tax partnership), subject to the additional tax and administrative complexities discussed below.

Tax Consequences of Granting a Vested Profits Interest

Revenue Procedure 93-27 provides a "safe harbor" for respecting a tax partnership equity grant as a non-taxable profits interest grant. Specifically, Revenue Procedure 93-27 allows a partnership interest grant to be valued based on what the recipient would receive if the partnership's assets were sold at fair market value and then the proceeds were distributed in a complete liquidation of the partnership. This prevents the equity grant from being taxed to the recipient, for example, based on prospective value of the company. In order to be eligible for this safe harbor, the profits interest grant must satisfy the following requirements:

1. The profits interest recipient is granted the profits interest for the provision of services to or for the benefit of a partnership in a partner capacity or in anticipation of being a partner;
2. The profits interest is not related to a substantially certain and predictable stream of income;
3. The profits interest is not disposed of within two years following the date of grant; and
4. The profits interest is not a limited partnership interest in a publicly traded partnership within the meaning of Section 7704(b).

Even if these safe harbor requirements are not met so that Revenue Procedure 93-27 does not apply, it may be possible for a partnership interest grant to qualify as a non-taxable equity grant based on federal income tax common-law standards, although such qualification will be less certain.

Depending on the particular format and features of the applicable operating agreement of the LLC issuing the profits interest, it may be advisable or essential that the LLC revalue or "book up" the Section 704(b) book-for-tax capital accounts of its members to reflect the fair market value of the LLC's assets as of immediately before the profits interest grant. This capital account "book up" may be necessary to ensure that the recipient does not participate in pre-grant value of the LLC, a threshold issue for profits interest qualification.

Neither the LLC nor any preexisting LLC member receives a compensation deduction attributable to the grant of a valid profits interest.

Tax Consequences of Granting an Unvested Profits Interest

An unvested profits interest may be treated as being received on the date of grant rather than on the date of vesting. Under Revenue Procedure 2001-43, neither the grant of a profits interest nor the later vesting of the interest is a taxable event for the recipient, the LLC or the LLC members as long as (1) the recipient is treated as an owner from the date of grant, (2) members of the LLC do not take any deduction (as wages, compensation, or otherwise) for the fair market value of the interest; and (3) all other conditions of Revenue Procedure 93-27 are satisfied. It is nonetheless advisable that a recipient of an unvested profits interest file a Section 83(b) election upon its receipt of such an interest.

The grant of an unvested profits interest, so long as it complies with the requirements of Revenue Procedures 93-27 and 2001-43, should generally be treated identically to the grant of a vested profits interest.

New Section 1061

Enacted with the Tax Cuts and Jobs Act of 2017, for tax years beginning on or after January 1, 2018, new Section 1061 increases the holding period requirement to three years for capital gain with respect to any "applicable partnership interest" to qualify for preferential long-term capital gains rates. For this purpose, an "applicable partnership interest" is generally an interest in a partnership that is granted in exchange for services provided to the partnership in any "applicable trade or business," which consists of raising or returning capital, and either investing in, disposing of or developing "specified assets." Specified assets include securities, commodities, real estate held for rental or investment, cash or cash equivalents, options or derivative contracts regarding any of such listed assets, or an interest in a partnership to the extent of the partnership's interest in such listed assets. Section 1061 does not apply to any capital interest in the partnership that provides a right to share in partnership capital commensurate with the amount of capital contributed (determined at the time of receipt of the partnership interest), or the value of such an interest subject to tax under Section 83 upon the receipt or vesting of the interest.

The scope of Section 1061 as enacted is currently uncertain, and hopefully forthcoming government guidance will clarify this new provision. LLCs and their current and prospective profits interest (and capital interest) recipients should be mindful of the new Section 1061 holding period requirements.

Options

A compensatory option granted by an LLC entitles a recipient to purchase LLC interests at a later date for a purchase price that is typically at least equal to the fair market value of the LLC interests as of the grant date. An option holder is generally not an equity holder for federal tax law purposes with respect to the underlying LLC interest until the date of exercise. In general, there is no taxable event on the date of grant of an option. When the recipient exercises an option, the recipient will recognize ordinary income in an amount equal to the excess of the fair market value of the purchased interests at the time of exercise over the exercise price. The tax treatment of an exercise of a compensatory option to the issuing LLC and the preexisting members generally mirrors the treatment described above for the grant of fully vested capital interests (subject to the same uncertainty).[18]

---

18. Prop. Reg. § 1.721-1(b)(3) (2005).

When a recipient sells the LLC interests acquired upon the exercise of an option, so long as the recipient holds the LLC interest in excess of a year, the recipient will be eligible to treat the associated taxable gain or loss as capital gain or loss, subject to any ordinary income attributable to "hot assets" held by the LLC and any required holding period impact of Section 1061, both as described above.

In practice, LLCs typically employ compensatory options in a manner similar to phantom equity. In most cases, the recipient does not exercise the option until an exit or liquidity event. Often, option recipients are rank-and-file employees that do not want the complications of being a partner in a tax partnership described below, and also want to avoid a "phantom income" event (i.e., tax recognition event that does not produce liquid proceeds from which to pay the tax) that would result from the exercise of the option. To avoid these issues, option holders accept that they will participate in the sale event at ordinary income rates rather than at capital gains rates.

Phantom Unit Rights and Phantom Unit Appreciation Plans

Unit rights plans and unit appreciation rights plans can be structured as cash compensation or bonus arrangements designed to track or mimic the economic rights of equity in an LLC without being actual equity interests in the LLC. Phantom unit plans in an LLC are typically subject to performance- or service-based vesting requirements. They can be structured to provide the full value of underlying equity on a vesting or payment date, or alternatively may be based on the appreciation in value of the corresponding equity from the date of the award. If the arrangement complies with or is exempt from Section 409A, as described below, then the taxable income recognition event for the recipient (as ordinary income) and the associated LLC compensation deduction is generally deferred until amounts are paid under the plan.

As with LLC compensatory options, a phantom unit plan issued by an LLC tax partnership typically is a preferred incentive tool for rank-and-file employees who want to avoid the complications of being a partner in a tax partnership described below, notwithstanding the unavailability of potential capital gains benefits on an exit.

Impact of Section 409A on Equity Compensation in LLCs

Section 409A relates to the taxation of nonqualified deferred compensation plans and applies to equity-based incentives that are deemed to be deferred compensation or otherwise result in deferred compensation. Nonqualified deferred compensation is generally a promise between a service provider and service recipient made in one year to pay compensation in a future year. Unless an arrangement is exempt from Section 409A, it must comply with Section 409A, which requires, among other things, that the compensation be reflected in a written document and be paid only on Section 409A specified payment events. Section 409A specified payment events include:

5. Separation from service (i.e., termination of employment or service from the employer and all companies in its controlled group);[19]
6. The occurrence of a disability;[20]
7. Death;
8. A specific date or pursuant to a fixed schedule (e.g., payment in a lump sum in 2022 or payment in 10 annual installments commencing in 2022) under which neither the employer nor the employee can affect the timing of the payments after the dates are already specified;[21]
9. A change in the ownership or effective control of the corporation;[22] or

---

19. A "separation from service" for employees under Section 409A of the Code generally has occurred when the facts and circumstances indicate that there is no "reasonable anticipation" by the service recipient or the employee that any services would be performed after a specified date, or that the level of bona fide services after that date would permanently decrease to no more than 20% of the average level of the services that the employee performed over the prior 36 months. See Treas. Reg. § 1.409A-1(h).
20. See Treas. Reg. § 1.409A-3(i)(4).
21. See Treas. Reg. § 1.409A-3(i)(1).
22. See Treas. Reg. § 1.409A-3(i)(5).

10. The occurrence of an unforeseeable emergency.[23]

If the requirements of Section 409A are not met with respect to deferred compensation subject to Section 409A, the recipient will be required to include otherwise deferred compensation in taxable income as of the date on which the amounts are no longer subject to a substantial risk of forfeiture. In addition to this current income inclusion, the recipient will be required to pay a 20% penalty tax and additional interest on the amount required to be included in income.

The preamble to the final regulations issued under Section 409A provides that an LLC may treat the issuance of its equity, including options to purchase the equity, under the same principles governing corporations' issuance of stock or options to purchase stock granted to employees or other service providers. Accordingly, until further guidance is provided, Section 409A apparently should apply to partnership equity in the same way it applies to stock in a corporation.

As more fully explained below, capital interests and profits interests are generally not subject to Section 409A. Options that are granted with an exercise price below fair market value of the underlying interests on the date of grant will be subject to Section 409A and must be structured to comply with the restrictive payment timing rules. If structured properly, phantom equity may not be considered to be deferred compensation and thus not subject to Section 409A.

Capital Interests and Profits Interests

Profits interests in a tax partnership (whether or not subject to vesting) are generally not subject to Section 409A because they are property subject to Section 83 and are not treated as deferred compensation for purposes of the Section 409A. Similarly, capital interests in a tax partnership (whether or not subject to vesting), if treated in accordance with the proposed regulations described above, should be property subject to Section 83 and not treated as Section 409A deferred compensation. These interests do not provide for a deferral of income beyond the vesting date, and are often treated as owned on the date of grant

---

23. See Treas. Reg. § 1.409A-3(i)(3).

if they are granted fully vested or if the recipient makes an election under Section 83(b).

Options

Since an option provides the recipient with the right to purchase the issuing company's interests at a later, unspecified date, an option is regarded as deferred compensation under Section 409A unless it is structured to be exempt from Section 409A. In general, an option may be exempt from Section 409A if (1) the option is granted on a class of interest that is analogous to a corporation's common stock; (2) the underlying equity does not carry distribution preferences; (3) except in limited circumstances, the underlying equity is not subject to a mandatory repurchase obligation or a put or call right where the obligation or right is based on a measure other than the fair market value of the stock; (4) the option is granted by the entity for which the recipient provides services, or any other entity in a chain of entities in which each entity has a controlling interest in another entity in the chain, ending with the entity that has a controlling interest in the entity for which the recipient performs direct services on the date of grant; (5) the option does not have another deferral feature; and (6) the option is granted with an exercise price at or above the fair market value of the underlying interest on the date of grant.[24]

Because an option is designed to allow the recipient to exercise the option for a period of time after the option becomes exercisable and before the option terminates (usually within 10 years following the date of grant), most options are intended to be exempt from Section 409A. If an option were subject to Section 409A, it would have to be designed so that it is exercisable only on one of the six Section 409A specified payment events set forth above. This would generally defeat one of the main advantages on an option, which is that the recipient can control the timing of tax consequences of exercise by choosing when to exercise the option. If an option is subject to, and not exempt from, Section 409A, the option recipient must include in income the excess of the fair market value of the equity on the last day of the year in which the option vests (or, if the option was exercised in the year of vesting,

---

24. See Treas. Reg. § 1.409A-1(b)(5).

on the date of exercise), over the exercise price, plus a 20% penalty tax on that amount, plus interest.

As noted above, in addition to meeting many other requirements, for an option to be exempt from Section 409A, the option must be granted with an exercise price at or above its fair market value as of the grant date. This particular requirement is one that necessitates that the LLC perform or obtain a valuation and, in practice, is the Section 409A requirement that many LLCs struggle to meet. Under Section 409A, the fair market value of the equity of a privately held company underlying the option must be based on an application of a reasonable valuation method. This valuation method takes into account all relevant facts and circumstances. The regulations under Section 409A list relevant factors to consider for a reasonable valuation method, including but not limited to:

- The value of the tangible and intangible assets of the corporation;
- The present value of future cash flows;
- The market value of stock or equity interests in similar corporations or entities engaged in substantially similar business;
- Recent arm's-length transactions involving the sale or transfer of the corporation's stock; and
- Other relevant factors, such as control premiums or minority discounts, and whether the valuation method is used for other purposes that have a material economic effect on the company, its equityholders, or its creditors.[25]

The IRS has also established certain "safe harbors" for testing the reasonableness of a private company's valuation method. If a company does not use a safe harbor method, and the IRS later challenges the valuation, then the burden falls on the company to show that its valuation determination was reasonable. If (1) the IRS proves that the valuation determination was not reasonable and (2) the exercise price is determined to be less than the fair market value on the date of grant, the option will be subject to the provisions of Section 409A. To avoid being subject

---

25. See Treas. Reg. § 1.409A-1(b)(5)(iv).

to Section 409A due to a flawed valuation method, companies should consider adopting one of the following safe harbor valuation methods:

1. A valuation established by an independent appraisal that meets certain prescribed statutory standards under the Code and applicable Treasury regulations, with the appraised value to be as of a date not more than 12 months before the relevant grant date, provided that no material changes have occurred that would increase the value over the 12-month period.

2. A valuation formula that, if used as a non-lapse restriction under Section 83, would be considered to produce a fair market value under Section 83.

3. For an illiquid stock that is (a) not subject to any non-lapse right to sell or purchase, or obligation (other than a first refusal right) and (b) issued by a startup corporation that has no trade or business that it has conducted for a period of 10 years or more, a written valuation report by an individual with sufficient knowledge, experience, and skill in evaluating illiquid stock of a startup corporation, which takes into account the valuation factors listed above. The report does not have to be prepared by an appraisal firm.

Private companies now regularly obtain a formal appraisal from an outside valuation firm to support the grant of options being exempt from Section 409A under the first exception listed immediately above. The cost for these valuation analyses is relatively minimal compared to the tax penalties associated with granting a noncompliant option, so this safe harbor valuation method has become increasingly popular.

Phantom Unit Rights and Phantom Unit Rights Appreciation Plans

Unit plans also need to be structured so that they comply with or are exempt from Section 409A. If the phantom equity plan is properly structured, the employee is subject to taxation when income is received under the arrangement. The LLC will also receive a deduction at the time of payment.

To be exempt from Section 409A, phantom unit plans should be structured and administered to meet the "short-term deferral" exemption. The "short-term deferral" rule excludes from deferred compensation those payments that by their terms must be received on or before the 15th day of the third month, following the later of either the end of the calendar year or the LLC's fiscal year in which phantom equity is no longer subject to a substantial risk of forfeiture. For example, if the phantom equity arrangement vests or otherwise is no longer subject to the risk of forfeiture in the year 2020 and the LLC's fiscal year is the calendar year, all bonus payments must be made by March 15, 2021.

If the award is structured to provide a one-time lump-sum payment upon or within 30 days following a recipient's termination of employment without cause, the payment will be made within the short-term deferral period by definition and thus be exempt from Section 409A. However, if the award is structured to provide a series of payments over a specified period of time, seeking an exemption from Section 409A could be more complicated, and the arrangement may need to comply with the restrictive payment events set forth under Section 409A, as described above.

Other Considerations

Employee/Partner Classification Issues

One of the potential complexities of granting equity compensation to employees of an LLC classified as a partnership for tax purposes is that the IRS takes the position that a member cannot also be an employee of the LLC.[26] Instead, once an employee owns an equity interest in an LLC, the individual is treated as a partner, and (1) the member should receive only a Schedule K-1, and not a Form W-2; (2) the member's salary will likely be treated as a partnership "guaranteed payment"; (3) the LLC should not withhold income taxes or make employment tax payments attributable to member payments; (4) the member must pay estimated taxes quarterly; (5) the member cannot participate in certain tax-advantaged benefit plans; (6) the member must pay self-employment taxes on its share of LLC income as self-employment income; and (7)

---

26. Rev. Rul. 69-184, 1969-1 C.B. 256; T.D. 9766 (May 3, 2016).

the member likely will be required to file tax returns in all jurisdictions in which the LLC files tax returns.

This means that an LLC member, such as a recipient of a capital interest or a profits interest, will be subject to self-employment taxes on its share of income generated by the LLC's activities. The tax partner status of the recipient also limits the recipient's tax advantages with respect to employee benefits, health insurance, and other fringe benefits. For example, being a partner affects the recipient's ability to exclude from income the health insurance premiums paid by the LLC on the recipient's behalf. As a member, the recipient also cannot participate in "cafeteria plans" (a reimbursement plan governed by Section 125, which allows employees to contribute a certain amount of their gross income to designated accounts before taxes are calculated).

In 2016, the IRS reinforced its historical position on this issue by issuing temporary regulations addressing tax partnership/disregarded entity tiered structures.[27] These temporary regulations clarify that an individual may not be a partner in one entity and an employee in another entity in a structure in which a partnership owns a disregarded entity. Therefore, for an LLC classified as a partnership that has one or more wholly owned subsidiaries that are disregarded entities, partners in the LLC cannot be treated as employees of the subsidiaries and vice versa.

In general, once a member of an LLC, the member's tax filings and other compliance responsibilities may become more complicated and costly, which should be considered seriously by both the LLC and the potential member before an LLC grants a capital interest or profits interest to an employee. Many employees, particularly those who are not in senior management, do not want to be subjected to the additional complexities that come along with being a member of an LLC. For these reasons, options, which can be structured to allow the employee and the employer to control the timing of whether and when the employee becomes a member of an LLC, or phantom unit plans, which have no prospect for the employee to become a member, may be preferable, albeit at the "cost" of not being able to treat any portion of their income or gain in an exit or liquidity event as capital gains.

---

27. Treas. Reg. § 301.7701-2T; T.D. 9766 (May 3, 2016).

There are some potential organizational structures that can be put into place to allow recipients of LLC interests to remain W-2 employees, which is beyond the scope of this chapter. Please see chapter 4 for a brief discussion of some of these structures.

Securities Law Considerations

Typically, when a company issues securities, the Securities and Exchange Commission (SEC) requires that the securities be registered with the SEC unless the transaction qualifies for an exemption from registration. Rule 701 of the Securities Act of 1933, as amended, is generally the exemption LLCs may use to grant equity compensation to its service providers without registering the equity with the SEC. Under Rule 701, private companies can offer their own securities to their employees or professional advisors without having to register the securities. An exemption from the registration requirement means that companies do not need to make SEC filings or pay any federal filing fees. However, companies are still required to comply with state securities laws, and anti-fraud, civil liability, or other provisions of federal securities laws. Issuing companies should not equate the exemption from SEC registration with an exemption from other relevant regulations.

Rule 701 Requirements

Rule 701 requires that all offers and sales of securities be included in a written compensatory benefit plan or a written compensation contract. Companies hoping to take advantage of Rule 701 need to satisfy several additional conditions:

1. The issuer cannot offer the securities to raise capital;
2. The aggregate sales (not offerings) of stocks during any consecutive 12-month period must *not* exceed the greater of (a) $1,000,000; (b) 15% of the total assets of the issuer (or of the issuer's parent company if the issuer is a wholly owned subsidiary); or (c) 15% of the outstanding amount of the class of securities being offered and sold;
3. The issuer must deliver to investors a copy of a compensatory benefit plan or a contract; and

4. For sales over $10 million during any consecutive 12-month period, the issuer must provide relevant disclosures to investors regarding (a) a copy of the summary plan description required by the Employee Retirement Income Security Act of 1974 (ERISA); (b) a summary of the material terms of the plan if the plan is not subject to ERISA; (c) information about the risks associated with the investment; and (d) a parent company's financial statements if the issuer is a wholly owned subsidiary.[28]

Additionally, there are special requirements for consultants and advisors purchasing or being granted securities. Offers and sales to consultants and advisors must be made for compensatory purposes only, not for other purposes, such as capital-raising transactions or promotion of the issuer's securities. The consultants and advisors must be natural persons providing bona fide services at the time of the offer.

Rule 701 Calculations and Timing

The aggregate sales price used in this provision reflects the sum of all cash, property, notes, cancellation of debt, or other considerations received or to be received by the issuer for the sale of the securities. The maximum total limit is based on actual sales, not simply offers. All options granted during any consecutive 12-month period are counted as part of the aggregate sales; options must be valued based on the exercise price of the option. Under Rule 701, the timing of calculating the sales price of securities is particularly important. As for options, the aggregate sales price should be calculated based on when an option grant is made (without regard to when the option becomes exercisable). With respect to other forms of securities, the calculation is made on the date of sale. With respect to deferred compensation or similar plans, the calculation is made when the irrevocable election to defer is made.[29]

Alternative Exemptions: "Accredited Investor" Exemption

If a Rule 701 exemption is not available, there are other exemptions an LLC can consider, such as under the accredited investor exceptions

---

28. 17 C.F.R. § 230.701 (2008).
29. Id.

under Regulation D of the Securities Act. The rules are based on facts and circumstances and require consultation with an expert who understands the securities laws.

State Securities Laws Considerations

Many states have exemptions similar to Rule 701 or require an offering to meet the requirements of Rule 701. For example, California eliminated several requirements that limited the ability to offer and sell securities, provided that issuing companies comply with Rule 701.[30] California used to strictly limit the total number of securities issuable under a plan. Now, companies can issue securities that are more than 30% of the outstanding securities of the companies. California also expanded the definition of persons eligible to receive stock options to be consistent with Rule 701 by including officers, advisors, and partners. Moreover, issuers do not have to provide annual financial statements to compensatory benefit plan participants if the issuers comply with Rule 701. As illustrated by California's state securities laws, state law exemptions resemble the requirement of Rule 701. Such similarities denote the importance of a thorough understanding of and compliance with Rule 701.

Many states require filings with their departments of securities or corporations in order to perfect the exemption. There is often an associated filing fee. Therefore, issuing companies should check with their state authorities to assure that all the procedural steps and state-specific requirements are satisfied.

Conclusion

Over the past few decades, the use of an LLC to conduct a privately held business has exploded and often now is the default organizational form for conducting an eligible business. The tax law applying to LLCs has mirrored the corporate law flexibility for this organizational form, whereby the LLC may generally determine how it and its owners will be taxed. Providing a service provider with LLC equity compensation can often be complicated, but has the potential to provide meaningful benefits for the LLC and the recipient if properly considered and implemented.

---

30. California Corporations Code § 25102(o).

Chapter 4

Allowing Holders of LLC Equity Interests to Be Treated As Employees

Wells Miller

Since 1969 the Internal Revenue Service (IRS) has taken the position that partners in a partnership, which includes holders of LLC capital and profits interests, cannot also be employees of the partnership.[1] As discussed under "Earned Income and Availability of Tax-Favored Fringe Benefits" in chapter 3 of this book, allowing partners to participate in employee benefit plans on the same terms as employees, or in plans that are available only to employees, risks disqualifying those plans, potentially causing adverse tax consequences to the plan sponsor and plan participants.

In the past, some employers who wished to allow holders of LLC equity interests to participate in employee-only plans set up a two-tiered structure in which employees were employed at an operating LLC while being granted equity interests in a holding LLC (figure 4-1).

Employers who adopted the above approach took the position that, although the operating LLC was a disregarded entity for federal tax purposes because it had only one member, the holding LLC was a separate partnership for purposes of employment taxes and withholding. This position was based on a reading of the entity classification

---

1. Revenue Ruling 69-184.

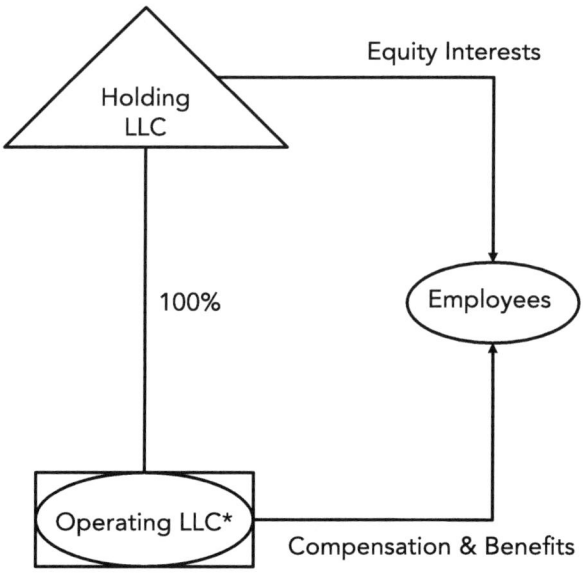

Figure 4-1

(also known as "check-the-box") regulations[2] that many practitioners felt was a stretch. Those that took this position often made a secondary argument: that the IRS had little incentive to challenge these arrangements because the affected individuals were paid on a W-2 and subject to income tax withholding (unlike partners) and that the revenue benefit of withholding outweighed any technical fault of allowing these individuals to participate in employee-only benefit plans.

Two recent developments have caused most employers to reconsider these arguments. First, in 2016, the IRS issued regulations that not only undermined the argument based on the check-the-box regulations but also explicitly rejected that approach in the preamble.[3] Second, a provision in the Tax Cuts and Jobs Act passed in December 2017 now allows a deduction to the owners of certain LLCs of up to 20% of the income allocated to the owners, but under some circumstances not in excess of 50% of the W-2 wages paid by the LLC. As a result, treating

---

2. Treas. Reg. 301.7701-2(c)(2)(iv)
3. Internal Revenue Bulletin 2016-21, TD 9766.

a partner as an employee, which includes paying them on a W-2, can have tax benefits for the owners of the LLC and gives the IRS a greater incentive to challenge such treatment.

Potential Structuring Solutions

Some employers have attempted to vary the above structure by issuing a small interest (generally 1%, although there are arguments for smaller percentages) in the operating LLC to a corporation formed by the holding LLC (figure 4-2).

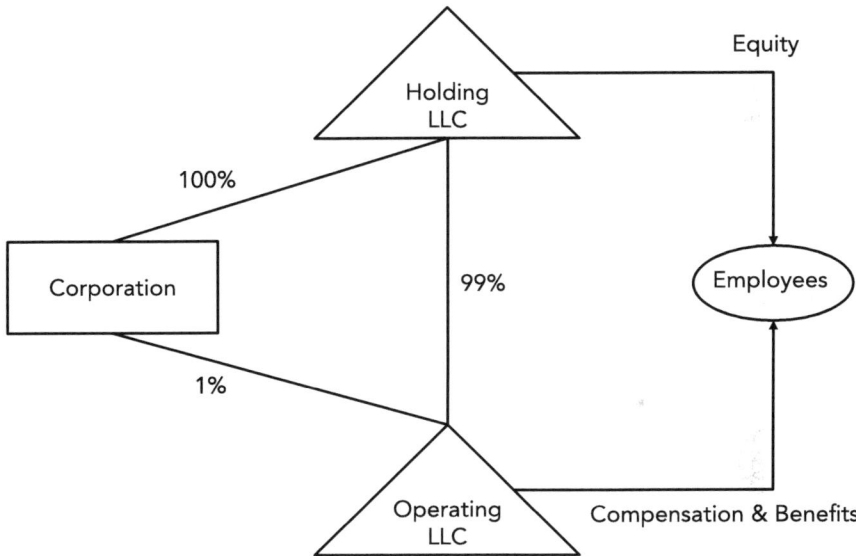

Figure 4-2

This structure is similar to the one described above, but in this case the ownership of the corporation should cause the operating LLC to be treated as a separate partnership, not a disregarded entity, and so would allow individuals to hold equity interests in the holding LLC while still being treated as employees of the operating LLC. While this approach involves additional annual maintenance costs (including two additional tax returns, one for the new corporation and the other for the formerly disregarded LLC now treated as a separate partnership), it would allow holders of LLC equity interests to participate in all employee benefit plans of their employer while also maximizing W-2 wages and therefore maximizing the amount of the deduction available under the Tax Cuts and Jobs Act.

Other employers have chosen to instead create a separate partnership to hold an interest in the operating LLC and to issue equity interests (see figure 4-3).

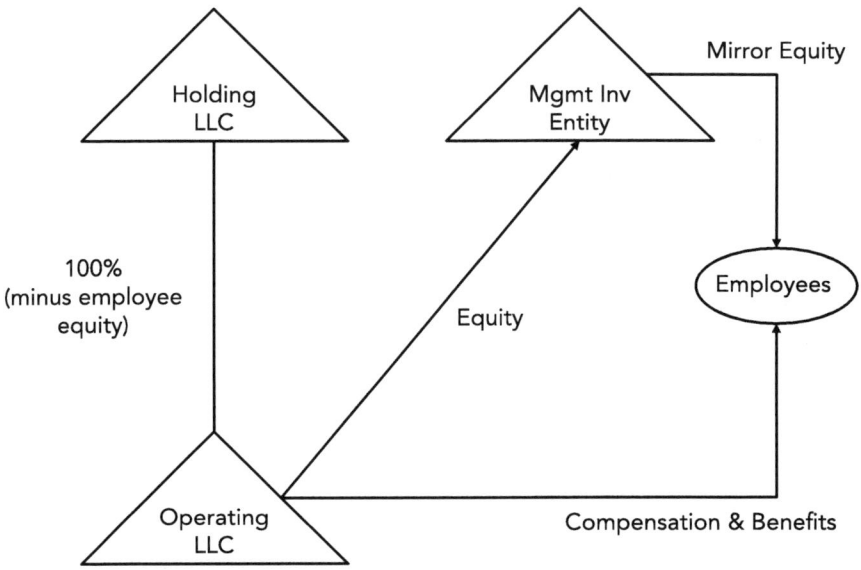

Figure 4-3

Under this approach, the operating LLC grants the equity interest not to the employee directly but instead to another partnership (often called a "management investment entity"). The employee is then granted equity interests in the management investment entity (rather than in the operating LLC), which mirror the equity interest granted by the operating LLC to the management investment entity. The intent is that, because the employees own an interest in the management investment entity, not the operating LLC, and because the operating LLC is no longer a disregarded entity (because it is owned by both the holding LLC and the management investment entity), the employees will be treated as employees of the operating LLC and partners in the management investment entity.

Note that while there are arguments supporting the structures described above, both might be challenged by the IRS as having no non-tax business purpose behind the corporation or the management investment entity. It is not clear whether a court is likely to agree, but many practitioners believe that past Tax Court rulings provide more support for respecting the existence of the corporation than for respecting the management investment entity.

Chapter 5

Accounting for Equity Compensation in an LLC

Alan Nadel

The limited liability company (LLC) has become a common form of business organization in the U.S. only within the past 30 years. While those who establish accounting standards have paid much attention to equity compensation, their focus has been primarily on corporations rather than other forms of legal entities, such as LLCs and partnerships. It has been quite common for decades to provide equity interests to employees, particularly executives, as a means of providing incentive and long-term compensation. Because LLCs have been introduced only relatively recently, the accounting literature applicable to equity compensation does not specifically address these types of entities. Nevertheless, the general language of the relevant accounting literature makes clear that it is appropriate to apply the same equity compensation accounting rules to other entities as those applicable to corporations.

Before getting into the specific rules applicable to equity compensation, it is first important to identify which set of rules we should be looking to. In the U.S., accounting for business transactions is covered under generally accepted accounting principles (GAAP). Virtually any transaction in American business is specifically addressed by one (and sometimes more than one) of the GAAP rules, including those for executive and employee pay programs. GAAP guidelines are developed primarily by the Financial Accounting Standards Board (FASB). All companies in the U.S. must follow GAAP regardless of whether they are publicly traded.

The FASB derives its authority from the Sarbanes-Oxley Act and the Securities and Exchange Commission (SEC). It is an independent board, but receives significant input from the SEC. Outside the U.S., accounting rules generally are established by the International Accounting Standards Board (IASB). The IASB establishes international financial reporting standards (IFRS) that have been adopted in more than 100 countries around the world. Although there has been considerable discussion in the U.S. about transitioning U.S. accounting standards from GAAP to IFRS, any changeover appears unlikely at this point. Consequently, U.S. companies continue to be subject to the rules of GAAP. While the rules of IFRS are similar to those of GAAP, notable differences exist between the two and may affect company stock-based programs if the U.S. eventually moves to IFRS.

Before 1995, the applicable accounting rules for equity compensation in the U.S. were dictated by Accounting Principles Board Opinion No. 25, *Accounting for Stock Issued to Employees* ("APB 25"). Recognizing that those accounting rules were developed for the simpler equity compensation programs of the early 1970s, the FASB decided to develop more comprehensive rules for equity compensation programs. It issued Statement of Financial Accounting Standards No. 123, *Accounting for Stock-Based Compensation* ("FAS 123"), in 1995. Under pressure from the business community, however, the FASB drafted FAS 123 to allow employers to choose whether they used the accounting of APB 25 or FAS 123. Most companies chose to continue using the older accounting rules under APB 25, whereby no expense was recognized for most stock options, and companies could simply disclose the effect of FAS 123 in their financial statement footnotes. When the economic environment changed significantly, the FASB revised the 1995 rules and made them mandatory for all companies under rules issued in late 2004, Statement of Financial Accounting Standards No. 123 (revised 2004), *Share-Based Payment* ("FAS 123R"). In 2009, the FASB introduced a new codified system for accounting standards. The portions of FAS 123R relating to equity payments for employees became Accounting Standards Codification Topic 718 ("ASC 718"), and the parts of FAS 123R relating to nonemployees became Accounting Standards Codification Subtopic 505-50 ("ASC 505-50").

Applicable Accounting

The rules of ASC 718 made significant changes to the accounting practices that almost all companies were following until 2005. Unlike the intrinsic value rules of APB 25, ASC 718 requires that the "fair value" of all equity compensation awards be recognized as an expense. The rules of ASC 718 are different from those under current GAAP for recognizing the cost of other assets and liabilities. Some of these changes are:

- Use of special valuation models for determining the cost of employee options to purchase employer equity
- Accrual patterns for recognizing the expense associated with vested awards
- Recognition of the income tax effects of equity awards
- Impact of performance-vested awards
- Modifications and other changes to outstanding equity awards

Although the rules of ASC 718 are geared toward corporate stock programs, they are just as relevant for equity interests that are granted to employees of unincorporated entities, including LLCs. Not surprisingly, certain adjustments must be made. In some LLC companies, employees are allowed to purchase an equity interest in the LLC. If the cost of that capital interest in the LLC is on the same terms (e.g., price) as for other investors in the LLC, then the employee's acquisition of the capital interest likely would not be treated as a compensatory one. ASC 718 would not be applicable, and the LLC would recognize no compensation expense. On the other hand, the grant (at less than the full cost) of a capital interest in the LLC generally would be subject to the expense recognition rules of ASC 718.

As discussed in previous chapters, employees in an LLC frequently receive a profits interest in the company rather than a capital interest. This allows the employees to share in the future profits of the business and receive a cash payment (either annually or on a deferred basis) rather than gain an ownership interest in the company that may increase in value over time. As discussed further below, the accounting for a profits interest generally is different from that for a capital interest.

Measurement

The first step in determining the accounting for an LLC interest is to measure the total amount of that expense. This may differ among the various types of LLC ownership interests, which are discussed in chapters 2 and 3 of this book.

Capital Interest

A capital interest in an LLC is similar to restricted stock in a corporation. In both cases the employee has an ownership interest in the capital or equity of the organization. Consequently, the accounting for both is similar. The employer must recognize an expense for the fair value of the capital interest that the employee is receiving for services rendered. In the case of a publicly traded company, the fair value generally is equal to the traded value of the stock or unit as determined by the public markets. Because most LLCs are privately held, however, determining fair value is more difficult. One indicator of fair value would be a reference to a recent similar transaction for a capital interest that was purchased by an unrelated third party. In the absence of such a purchase, it may be necessary to obtain an appraisal or other determination of value from an independent professional. In some cases, it may be helpful to establish a formula value that would be used for purposes of buying and selling capital interests in the LLC.

In 2011 the American Institute of Certified Public Accountants (AICPA) revised its Practice Aid to guide privately held companies with the valuation of their equity securities issued for purposes of employee compensation. The AICPA Practice Aid indicates that the valuation of these equity securities should be conducted using any of three acceptable valuation methods:

- Market
- Income (e.g., discounted cash flows)
- Asset

Although independent appraisers have used other commonly accepted valuation methods, only these three valuation methodologies meet the guidelines established in the Practice Aid. Also, although all of the methodologies detailed in the Practice Aid are used by valuation specialists, the Practice Aid indicates a preference for different methods based on various characteristics or other criteria specific to each company's circumstances.

Furthermore, the Practice Aid provides a hierarchy of valuation methodologies to indicate a preference for the type of valuation private companies should use. Preferably, the valuation should be conducted by an unrelated valuation specialist contemporaneously with the issuance of the compensatory equity. If that is not possible, the next preferred approach is a retrospective valuation by an unrelated valuation specialist. The least preferred method for valuing the securities is a valuation established by a "related party valuation specialist."

Valuations that are performed consistent with the guidelines detailed in the AICPA Practice Aid will be more likely to meet the approval of the company's auditors. With respect to private companies that undergo an initial public offering (IPO), the SEC has accepted valuations of employee equity using the AICPA Practice Aid and has not challenged these valuations. This is a significant departure from the SEC's previous practice of challenging the valuation of employee equity issued in the year prior to an IPO under its "cheap stock" theory. This often resulted in companies recognizing an additional compensation expense at the time of the IPO in order to gain SEC approval. Instead, companies following the guidelines of the AICPA Practice Aid for the valuation of employee equity generally will not be challenged by the SEC in this regard. In contrast, companies that do not use the AICPA Practice Aid may face greater SEC scrutiny, including cheap stock challenges before an IPO.

Option to Purchase a Capital Interest

The grant of an option to purchase a capital interest in the LLC will be treated similarly to a stock option in a corporation, which allows an employee to buy corporate stock at a time of his or her choosing within a specified time frame and at agreed-upon terms. Unlike the previous accounting rules of APB 25, ASC 718 requires the use of special valuation models for determining the value of the option. The LLC may choose to use a closed-form valuation model (e.g., Black-Scholes) or an open-form approach such as the polynomial model. The FASB has no preference which formula the employer chooses, provided that it is applied consistently. Most companies use the Black-Scholes formulation because of its simplicity. Both approaches require the use of six valuation assumptions:

- Fair value of the underlying equity (e.g., capital interest)
- Exercise price of the option
- Life or term of the option
- Prevailing risk-free interest rate
- Volatility of the price of the underlying capital interest
- Dividend yields of the capital interest, if any

Each of these assumptions must be calculated or estimated by the company. Under the Black-Scholes approach, each of the valuation factors is assumed to remain constant throughout the life of the option. In contrast, an open-form model allows the employer to assume that the valuation assumptions will change over the life of the option as well as to consider other factors (e.g., the probability of employee turnover) that may affect the value of the option.

Each of the valuation assumptions is determined for an LLC similar to the way it would be for a corporation. The most difficult assumption, however, is the determination of volatility. Assuming the LLC is a privately held company, it is difficult or impractical to measure the expected volatility of an LLC unit. Instead, the LLC is required to measure its options to purchase a capital interest based on a value determined by using the historical volatility of an appropriate industry sector index of similar companies instead of the expected volatility of an LLC unit price.

Profits Interest

Unlike the capital interest in an LLC, a profits interest provides only for a share of future income of the LLC. Although the terms of the profits interest may allow the employee to sell his or her interest in the LLC, it does not represent any ownership of the underlying capital or equity of the company. It is merely a right to a future cash payment based on company profits. ASC 718 addresses situations in which employee awards are settled in cash rather than an ownership interest in the business. It specifically provides for "liability" accounting in such cases.

The accounting rules allow the private company to make a "policy decision" about how to account for liability awards. The company may use either fair value or intrinsic value for award valuation purposes. Regardless of which approach is used, the profits interest is valued at the grant date (similar to the treatment of capital interests). Furthermore, in each subsequent accounting period the profits interest is subject to mark-to-market treatment until the award is settled. The result is that the company ultimately recognizes an expense for all cash payments made to the employee while the employee holds the profits interest rather than fixing the expense at the initial date of grant.

Carried Interest

As noted in chapter 2, another form of compensation that is common to many LLCs (particularly private equity and hedge funds) is the "carried interest," a perceived form of equity. A carried interest provides the employee with the right to share in the profits of the LLC. In fact, a carried interest is just a type of profits interest. In some cases a carried interest is nothing more than a bonus arrangement, whereas in others it may entitle the employee to an ongoing, predetermined portion of the LLC profits, calculated after all expenses have been paid. In other cases, a carried interest may be defined as a portion of the proceeds from the future sale of the company. Because carried interests have become a common form of employee compensation, they frequently are subject to vesting and/or performance conditions. They also may be subject to contingencies such as the company achieving a specified rate of return or having an "exit event" (i.e., undertaking an initial public offering or a sale of the company). Although the carried interest is not actually equity in the LLC, it can be designed in a manner that provides the holder with an ongoing right to future income and that can be sold or otherwise transferred to others, depending on its terms and the LLC's operating agreement. Because it is settled in cash, it is subject to the liability accounting treatment applicable to profits interests.

LLC Equity Appreciation Rights

As discussed above, phantom LLC units track periodic profits distributed by the LLC, similar to stock appreciation rights in a corporation. The employee receives no LLC ownership interest other than the right to receive periodic cash payments. Consequently, LLC equity appreciation rights will be accounted for in the same manner as profits interests using liability accounting.

Compensation Expense Accruals

Once the amount of compensation expense has been determined under equity accounting, the aggregate expense must be amortized over the employee's service period. This is usually the same as the vesting period. If the vesting occurs all at the end of the service period, the total expense is amortized on a level (straight-line) basis so that the same amount of expense is recognized each year during the service period.

If the employee gradually vests each year during the service period, the employer may choose either straight-line or multiple-option amortization. By using the multiple-option approach, the amount of the expense to be recognized each year is treated as a separate award and amortized accordingly. For example an award that vests ratably over three years is treated as a grant of three separate awards: an award vesting in one year, an award vesting in two years, and an award vesting in three years. Each year's award is expensed over its appropriate vesting period. The net result is an expense in the first year consisting of 100% of the first year's award, plus 50% of the second year's award, plus 33% of the third year's award. The second year expense is equal to 50% of the second year's award plus 33% of the third year's award. The third year expense would consist of only the remaining portion of the third year's award (i.e., 33%). Because of the front-loading effect of multiple-option amortization as well as its complexity, most companies use straight-line amortization.

Vesting Conditions

Under equity accounting, the basis for determining an employee's vesting in the award may affect the amount of expense recognized for that award. If the vesting is based on service or performance conditions, no compensation expense is recognized for awards that are forfeited as a result of termination of employment or performance conditions not achieved. Forfeitures are estimated at the time of grant, and the estimate is eventually trued up based on actual experience during the vesting period. Additionally, compensation expense attributable to forfeited awards that was recognized in prior periods is reversed in the period of forfeiture.

Under new FASB rules that became effective after 2017, private companies must make an accounting policy election concerning forfeitures. The LLC must decide whether to (1) continue to initially estimate (at grant date) the number of awards that will be forfeited and subsequently adjust the estimate when a change becomes probable, or (2) recognize forfeitures of capital awards as they occur. This election is made at the entity level so that it will apply to all equity awards granted by the LLC. If vesting is somehow tied to the value of the LLC (e.g., attainment of a predetermined unit value), no adjustments are made for forfeitures. Instead, the estimated forfeitures are one of the factors used in determining the value of the award. Because the typical LLC is not publicly traded, this provision is seldom seen in LLC awards.

Income Tax Benefit

Generally, most LLCs in the U.S. choose to be taxed as a partnership rather than as a corporation. As such, those LLCs do not benefit from any tax deductions associated with equity compensation. Instead, the LLC's owners (i.e., the unit holders) benefit from the tax deduction because of the pass-through nature of partnership income.

Under equity accounting, if the vesting or settlement of a capital interest is expected to produce a tax deduction for the LLC (presumably because the LLC elected to be taxed as a corporation), the benefit of that tax deduction must be taken into account in determining the net cost of the equity award. Because of the differences in the timing of an expense of an award (at grant) and the tax deduction for that award (vesting, exercise, or payout), determining the relevant amounts of the future tax deductions is more complicated. The tax benefit is calculated based on the grant date value of the equity award and the company's effective tax rate.

The FASB changed its rules concerning the income tax benefits associated with equity plans effective for years after 2017 for nonpublic companies. Before this change, companies were required to maintain a pool of unused tax benefits that would have been recognized under FAS 123 between 1995 and 2005. Furthermore, any additional tax benefits that arose after 2005 and were not included in income were to be added to the pool. This pool of unused tax benefits was used to offset shortfalls that occurred in later years when the actual tax benefit in any period was less than the expected tax benefit.

For periods commencing after 2017, new rules apply. Both excess tax benefits and tax deficiencies (shortfalls) are to be fully reflected in income tax expense in the company's current period income statement. A tax benefit should be recognized currently regardless of whether the benefit reduces taxes payable in the current period. Excess benefits and deficiencies may no longer be carried forward to future periods. Any unused tax benefits remaining in the pool when the new rules took effect will remain in additional paid-in capital in the company's balance sheet and may no longer be adjusted. The tax effects of exercised or vested awards should be reflected as discrete items in the period in which they occur.

Modifications

In the event that an award is subsequently modified, it is treated as the exchange of the original award for a new equity award. A modification is deemed to occur when there is a change in any of the award's terms or conditions. An additional compensation expense must be recognized for any incremental fair value of the new award over the fair value of the canceled award. Additionally, any remaining unrecognized compensation cost from the date of grant must also be recognized. Determinations of change in value must be measured in terms of fair value rather than intrinsic value. The measurement of additional compensation expense is based on the fair value of the equity award immediately before the modification and immediately after the modification. In no event may the total compensation expense be less than the fair value at the date of grant.

Based on recent changes by the FASB, the modification rules of ASC 718 will apply only when any of the following terms or conditions changes:

- Fair value (or calculated intrinsic value, if applicable)
- Vesting conditions
- Classification of the award as equity or liability

Some examples of modifications are:

- Accelerating or extending vesting of outstanding awards
- Changing performance targets
- Exchanges of equity awards in connection with a merger or an equity restructuring
- Inducements to terminate employment or retire early (e.g., extending the term of an option or an option exercise period)
- Repricing an equity instrument

Chapter 6

A Primer on Sharing Equity with Employees in Non-LLC Companies

Corey Rosen

This book focuses on equity compensation plans for limited liability companies that choose to be taxed as partnerships or sole proprietorships, but it is important to understand equity compensation in the context of C or S corporations as well for three reasons. First, if you do a web search for equity compensation plans in LLCs, most of the articles will say that it is a lot easier and often recommended to switch to S or C status instead because the rules and alternative approaches are simpler and more certain. Second, the concepts of sharing equity in an LLC generally parallel concepts in an S or C corporation. By understanding these more familiar concepts, it may be easier to see how their equivalents in LLCs work. Finally, if you choose to be taxed as an S or C corporation, you can use any of the plans described here.

For most LLCs that elect to not be taxed as a partnership, an S corporation is the logical choice. The tax treatment of S corporations and LLCs is similar in many ways. Both are pass-through entities, meaning there is no corporate-level tax. Instead, individual owners pay taxes on any profits and gains. While there are a number of differences, as explained in chapter 1, the key difference is that in an S corporation, distributions must be proportional to ownership, whereas an LLC can make distributions in other ways if it so chooses.

The first part of this chapter looks at individual equity plans; these plans can be used for selective or broad-based plans. The second part looks at plans that are designed to benefit most or all employees. This chapter focuses on plan design and tax issues. Securities law considerations are briefly discussed in a separate section, but because this is such a complex subject, they are not reviewed in any detail. Accounting issues are extremely complex and varied for different plans and are discussed only briefly here. For more information on accounting concerns, see the NCEO's books *Accounting for Equity-Based Compensation* (for individual equity plans and employee stock purchase plans) or *Leveraged ESOPs and Employee Buyouts* (for ESOPs).

Basic Forms of Individual Equity Plans in Conventional Corporations

There are four basic kinds of individual equity compensation plans in C or S corporations: stock options, restricted stock and restricted stock units, stock appreciation rights, and phantom stock. Many of these plans have variations as well. Each plan provides employees with some special consideration in price or terms. (This chapter does not cover simply offering employees the right to buy stock on the same terms any other investor would receive, or making unrestricted grants of shares.)

Stock options give employees the right to buy a number of shares at a price fixed at grant for a defined number of years into the future. *Restricted stock* (and its close relative *restricted stock units*) gives employees the right to acquire or receive shares, by gift or purchase, once certain restrictions, such as working a certain number of years or meeting a performance target, are met. *Phantom stock* pays a future cash bonus equal to the value of a certain number of shares. *Stock appreciation rights* provide the right to the increase in the value of a designated number of shares, usually paid in cash, but occasionally settled in shares (this is called a "stock-settled SAR").

Stock Options

A few key concepts help define how stock options work:

- *Exercise:* The purchase of stock with an option.

- *Exercise price:* The price at which the stock can be purchased. This is also called the *strike price*. In most plans, the exercise price is the current fair market value of the stock at the time the exercise is made.
- *Grant price:* How much the option holder must pay to exercise the option.
- *Spread:* The difference between the grant price and exercise price at the time of exercise.
- *Option term:* The amount of time the employee can hold the option before it expires.
- *Vesting:* The requirement, usually in years of service, that must be met for an option holder to be able to exercise an option.

A company grants an employee options to buy a stated number of shares at a defined grant price. The options vest over a period of time or once certain individual, group, or corporate goals are met. Once vested, the employee can exercise the option at the grant price at any time over the option term up to the expiration date. For instance, an employee might be granted the right to buy 1,000 shares at $10 per share. The options vest 25% per year over four years and have a term of 10 years. If the stock goes up, the employee will pay $10 per share to buy the stock. The difference between the $10 grant price and the exercise price is the spread. If the stock goes to $25 after seven years, and the employee exercises all options, the spread would be $15 per share.

Kinds of Options

Employee stock options are either incentive stock options (ISOs) or nonqualified stock options (NSOs). When an employee exercises a nonqualified stock option, the spread on exercise is taxable to the employee as ordinary income, even if the shares are not yet sold. A corresponding amount is deductible by the company. There is no legally required holding period for the shares after exercise, although the company may impose one. Any subsequent gain or loss on the shares after exercise is taxed as capital gains or losses.

An incentive stock option (ISO) enables an employee to (1) defer taxation on the option from the date of exercise until the date of sale of the underlying shares and (2) to pay tax at capital gains rates, rather than ordinary income tax rates, on the spread at exercise. Certain conditions must be met to qualify for ISO treatment:

1. The employee must hold the stock for at least one year after the exercise date or two years after the grant date, whichever is later.
2. Only $100,000 of stock options can become exercisable in any year. This is measured by the grant price of the options, not the exercise price. It means that only $100,000 in grant price value can vest (first become exercisable) in any one year. If there is overlapping vesting, such as would occur if options are granted annually and vest gradually, companies must track outstanding options to see if the amount that becomes vested under different grants would exceed $100,000 in grant value in any one year. Any amount exceeding $100,000 is treated as coming from an NSO.
3. The exercise price must be equal to at least 100% of the market price of the company's stock on the date of the grant.
4. Only employees can qualify for an ISO.
5. The option must be granted pursuant to a written plan that has been approved by shareholders, that specifies how many shares can be issued under the plan, and that identifies the class of employees eligible to receive the options. Options must be granted within 10 years of the date of the adoption of the plan.
6. The option cannot by its terms be exercisable more than 10 years after the date of the grant.
7. The employee cannot own, at the time of the grant, more than 10% of the voting power of all outstanding stock of the company, unless the exercise price is at least 110% of the market value of the stock on the date of the grant, and the option is not exercisable more than five years from the date of the grant.

If all the rules for incentive options are met at the time of exercise, then the transaction is called a "qualifying disposition," and the employee pays capital gains tax on the total increase in value at sale over the grant price. However, the spread on the option at exercise is a "preference item" for purposes of the alternative minimum tax (AMT). So even though the shares may not have been sold, the exercise requires the employee to add back the gain on exercise, along with other AMT preference items, to see if an alternative minimum tax payment is due.

The company does not take a tax deduction when there is a qualifying disposition. If, however, there is a disqualifying disposition, most often because the employee exercises and sells before meeting the required holding periods, the spread on exercise is taxable to the employee at ordinary income tax rates, and any capital appreciation on the ISO shares in excess of the market price on exercise of an ISO is taxed at capital gains rates. In this instance, the company may then deduct the spread on exercise.

Exercising an Option

There are four ways to exercise a stock option: cash, the exchange of existing shares (often called a stock swap), same-day sales, and their close relative, sell-to-cover sales (these latter two are often called cashless exercises, although that term actually includes other kinds of exercise methods described here as well). Any one company, however, may provide for just one or two of these alternatives. Private companies do not offer same-day or sell-to-cover sales, and they often restrict the exercise or sale of the shares acquired through exercise until the company is sold or goes public.

The most common form of exercise for an option in a closely held company is simply for the employee to pay cash for the shares. The employee might then have additional taxes due, depending on the kind of option. If the options are nonqualified, the employer might then have to withhold taxes on the spread from the employee's future paychecks, unless the employer can arrange to use some of the option shares to pay for this obligation, as would normally be the case in the kind of cashless transactions described below.

In a same-day sale, the employee works with a broker, usually one provided by the company. The company provides the broker with enough shares to cover the option exercise, the broker turns around and sells them, and the proceeds, minus the exercise price and any taxes due, go to the employee. Although called a "same-day" sale, the process can take up to three days. In a sell-to-cover exercise, the same approach is used, but the broker sells only enough shares to cover the exercise price and any taxes due, giving the employee the remaining value in shares.

In a stock swap, the employee simply exchanges existing shares for the option shares. For instance, if the employee has the right to buy 1,000 shares at $10 per share and the shares are now worth $25, the employee would exchange 400 shares the employee currently owns for the 1,000 shares. That's because the 400 shares the employee owns are worth $10,000. The employee would then get 600 shares from the option. If there are taxes due as well, then the employee might choose to turn in enough shares to cover the taxes as well, although this is not a common strategy. Stock swaps are more commonly used with incentive stock options where taxes do not have to be paid until the newly acquired shares are sold.

Accounting

Under rules for equity compensation plans that became effective in 2006, companies must calculate the present value of all option awards as of the date of grant and show this as a charge to compensation. The value should be adjusted based on vesting experience (so unvested shares do not count as a charge to compensation).

Restricted Stock

Restricted stock provides the employee with the right to purchase shares at fair market value or a discount, or simply grants shares to employees outright. However, the shares employees acquire are not really theirs yet—they cannot take possession of the shares until specified restrictions lapse. Most commonly, the restriction is that the employee works for the company for a certain number of years, often three to five. The time-based restrictions may pass all at once or gradually. Any restrictions could be imposed, however. The company could, for instance, restrict the shares until certain corporate, departmental, or individual performance goals are achieved. With restricted stock units (RSUs), employees do not actually buy or receive shares *until* the restrictions lapse. In effect, RSUs are like phantom stock settled in shares instead of cash.

While the shares are subject to restrictions, companies can choose whether to pay dividends, provide voting rights, or give the employee other benefits of being a shareholder. When employees are awarded the restricted stock, they have the right to make what is called a "Section 83(b)" election. If they make the election, they are taxed at ordinary income tax rates on the "bargain element" of the award at the time of grant. If the shares are simply granted to the employee, then the bargain element is their full value. If some consideration is paid, then the tax is based on the difference between what is paid and the fair market value at the time of the grant. If full price is paid, there is no tax. Any future increase in the value of the shares until they are sold is then taxed as capital gains, not ordinary income. If employees do not make the election, then there is no tax until the restrictions lapse, at which time ordinary income tax is due on the difference between the grant and exercise price. Subsequent changes in value are capital gains (or losses). Employees cannot make the Section 83(b) election for RSUs.

The employer gets a tax deduction only for amounts employees pay income tax on, regardless of whether a Section 83(b) election is made or not. A Section 83(b) election carries some risk. If the employee makes the election and pays tax, but the restrictions never lapse, the employee does not get the taxes paid refunded, nor does the employee get the shares.

Restricted stock accounting parallels option accounting in most respects. If the only restriction is vesting, companies account for restricted stock by first determining the total compensation cost at the time the award is made. So if the employee is simply given 1,000 restricted shares worth $10 per share, then a $10,000 cost is incurred. If the employee buys the shares at fair value, no charge is recorded; if there is a discount, that counts as a cost. The cost is then amortized over the period of vesting until the restrictions lapse. Because the accounting is based on the initial cost, companies with a low share price will find that a vesting requirement for the award means their accounting charge will be very low even if the stock price goes up.

If the award is more contingent, such as performance vesting, the value must be adjusted each year for the current stock price, then amortized over the estimated life of the award (the time estimated to meet the performance goal). Each year, the expected cost is amortized over the estimated remaining expected life. So if the stock is awarded at $10 and goes to $15 in the first year of an expected five-year term, then $15 x 1,000 x .20 is recorded ($3,000). If the price goes to $18 the next year, the calculation is $18 x 1,000 x .40 ($3,600). The prior $2,000 is subtracted from this amount, yielding a charge of $1,800 for that year.

Phantom Stock and Stock Appreciation Rights

Stock appreciation rights (SARs) and phantom stock are very similar plans. Both essentially are cash bonus plans, although some plans pay out the benefits in the form of shares. SARs typically provide the employee with a cash payment based on the increase in the value of a stated number of shares over a specific period of time. Phantom stock provides a cash or stock bonus based on the value of a stated number of shares, to be paid out at the end of a specified period of time. SARs may not have a specific settlement date; like options, the employees may have flexibility in when to choose to exercise the SAR. Phantom stock may pay dividends; SARs generally do not. When the payout is made, it is taxed as ordinary income to the employee and is deductible to the employer. Some phantom plans condition the receipt of the award on meeting certain objectives, such as sales, profits, or other targets. These plans often call their phantom stock "performance units."

Because SARs and phantom plans are essentially cash bonuses or are delivered in the form of stock that holders will want to cash in, companies need to figure out how to pay for them. Does the company just make a promise to pay or does it really put aside the funds? If the award is paid in stock, is there a market for the stock? If it is only a promise, will employees believe the benefit is as phantom as the stock? If it is in real funds set aside for this purpose, the company will be putting after-tax dollars aside instead of using them in the business. Many small, growth-oriented companies cannot afford to do this. The fund can also be subject to excess accumulated earnings tax. On the other hand, if employees are given shares, the shares can be paid for by capital markets if the company goes public or by acquirers if the company is sold.

If phantom stock or SARs are irrevocably promised to employees, it is possible the benefit will become taxable before employees actually receive the funds. A "rabbi trust," a segregated account to fund deferred payments to employees, may help solve the accumulated earnings problem, but if the company is unable to pay creditors with existing funds, the money in these trusts goes to them. Telling employees their right to the benefit is not irrevocable, or is dependent on some condition (working another five years, for instance), may prevent the money from being currently taxable, but it may also weaken employee belief that the benefit is real.

Finally, if phantom stock or SARs are intended to benefit most or all employees and defer some or all payment until termination or later, they may be considered a de facto "ERISA plan." ERISA (the Employee Retirement Income Security Act of 1974) is the federal law that governs retirement plans. It does not allow non-ERISA plans to operate like ERISA plans, so the plan could be ruled subject to all the constraints of ERISA. Similarly, if there is an explicit or implied reduction in compensation to get the phantom stock, there could be securities issues involved, most likely anti-fraud disclosure requirements. Plans designed just for a limited number of employees, or as a bonus for a broader group of employees that pays out annually based on a measure of equity, would most likely avoid these problems. Moreover, the regulatory issues are "gray areas"; it could be that a company could use a broad-based plan that pays over longer periods or at departure and not ever be challenged.

Phantom stock and SAR accounting is straightforward. These plans are treated in the same way as deferred cash compensation. As the amount of the liability changes each year, an entry is made for the amount accrued. A decline in value would create a negative entry. These entries are not contingent on vesting. In closely held companies, share value is often stated as book value. However, this can dramatically underrate the true value of a company, especially one based primarily on intellectual capital. Having an outside appraisal performed, therefore, can make the plans much more accurate rewards for employee contributions.

Employee Stock Purchase Plans

Millions of employees become owners in their companies through employee stock purchase plans (ESPPs). Many of these plans are organized under Section 423 of the tax code and thus are often called "Section 423" plans. Other ESPPs are "nonqualified" plans, meaning they do not have to meet the special rules of Section 423 and do not get any of the special tax treatment.

Under Section 423, companies must allow all employees to participate but can exclude those with less than two years' tenure, part-time employees, and highly compensated employees. All employees must have the same rights and privileges under the plan, although companies can allow purchase limits to vary with relative compensation (most do not do this, however). Plans can limit how much employees can buy, and the law limits it to $25,000 per year.

Section 423 plans operate by allowing employees to have deductions taken out of their pay on an after-tax basis. These deductions accumulate over an "offering period." At a specified time or times employees can choose to use these accumulated deductions to purchase shares, or they can get the money back. Plans can offer discounts of up to 15% on the price of the stock. Most plans allow this discount to be taken based on *either* the price at the beginning or end of the offering period (the so-called "look-back feature"). The offering period can last up to five years if the price employees pay for their stock is based on the share price at the end of the period or 27 months if it can be determined at an earlier point.

Plan design can vary in a number of ways. For instance, a company might allow employees a 15% discount on the price at the end of the offering period, but no discount if they buy shares based on the price at the beginning of the period. Some companies offer employees interim opportunities to buy shares during the offering period. Others provide smaller discounts. Offering periods also vary in length. NCEO studies, however, show that the large majority of plans have a look-back feature and provide 15% discounts off the share price at the beginning or end of the offering period. Most of the plans have a 12-month offering period, with six months the next most common.

The tax treatment of a Section 423 plan is similar to that of an incentive stock option plan. If employees hold the shares for two years after grant and one year after exercise, they pay ordinary income tax on the lesser of (1) the discount element as of the beginning of the offering period and (2) the amount by which the sale price exceeds the purchase price. Any additional gain is taxed as a long-term capital gain. The company gets no tax deduction, even on the discount. There is no withholding requirement on the gain on the employee purchase of shares.

If these rules are not met, employees pay ordinary income tax on the difference between the exercise price and the fair market value of the stock on the purchase date, plus long-term or short-term capital gains taxes on any increase in value over the purchase price. The company gets a tax deduction for the spread between the purchase price and the exercise price.

Nonqualified ESPPs usually work much the same way, but there are no rules for how they must be structured and no special tax benefits. The employee would pay tax on the discount as ordinary income *at the time the stock is purchased* and would pay capital gains on any subsequent gain.

ESPPs are found almost exclusively in public companies because the offering of stock to employees requires compliance with costly and complex securities laws. Closely held companies can, and sometimes do, have these plans, however. Offerings of stock only to employees can qualify for an exemption from securities registration requirements at the federal level, although they will have to comply with anti-fraud disclosure rules and, possibly, state securities laws as well. If they do offer stock in a stock purchase plan, it is highly advisable to obtain at least an annual appraisal.

ESPPs are very popular in public companies and some pre-IPO companies (where the plan starts before the IPO, and purchases are not made until after it) as they offer a benefit to employees and additional capital to companies. Any dilution resulting from the issuance of new shares to satisfy the purchase requests, or from the company repurchasing outstanding shares and reselling them at a discount, is usually so small that shareholders do not object. Rates of participation vary widely, with the median levels around 30% to 40% of eligible employees. Because most employees do not commit large amounts to these plans, and many do not participate at all, ESPPs should generally be seen as an adjunct to other employee ownership plans, not a means in themselves to create an ownership culture.

ESPPs are accounted for in the same way as options. Any discount offered counts as a compensation charge, and the present value of the option element must be calculated as an additional charge to income.

Securities Law Issues

If employees are given a right to purchase shares, the offer is subject to securities laws. See the "Securities Law Considerations" section at the end of chapter 3 for a discussion of these issues.

Chapter 7

Communicating with Employees About Equity

Corey Rosen

Companies usually create equity plans, at least in part, to attract, retain, and motivate employees. That makes sense. Companies that employ good people and have strong corporate cultures of employee engagement have a huge competitive edge. They are also in a buyer's market for employees, who will look on the company's culture with particular favor. Even in difficult times, companies that can maintain employee engagement are much more likely to survive, in part because engaged employees are more likely to come up with innovative ideas for saving money and generating new products.

One of the most important ways companies can maintain or build cultures of engagement is by linking their equity programs to a broader corporate culture that treats people like owners. Plan design matters as well—who gets equity, how much they get, when they get it, what triggers an award, and when it becomes liquid all can reinforce a shared sense of ownership or undermine it. An effective equity plan cannot simply be a potentially very lucrative carrot dangled in front of employees in the hopes they will make extraordinary efforts to help the company succeed. While a few exceptional companies do become the Googles and Microsofts that create legendary numbers of very wealthy employees, the usual story is far more modest, with equity being a welcome and even substantial added benefit, but nonetheless just one part of a three-legged stool of base pay, benefits, and equity that make up a good compensation package.

The research on employee ownership, employee turnover, corporate performance, and employee engagement is very consistent. Studies since the 1980s through a 2011 analysis published by the National Bureau of Economic Research of what is probably the largest data set ever compiled on employee attitudes, organizational culture, and organizational performance show that for shared ownership plans to work, they must both be communicated effectively and be linked to high-engagement management styles.[1] These include sharing corporate performance data, work teams, ad hoc committees, devolving decision-making to the lowest possible level, and other ways to help employees share ideas and information.

Effective communication helps people understand what they are getting, when they will get it, and what they need to do, individually and as members of the organization, to earn it. People will come away knowing the realistic benefits and rewards of equity in your company's specific environment, not in an imagined environment of stories they have heard about equity riches (or losses) in highly publicized (and thus by definition atypical) cases. High-involvement management allows employees to use the motivation the equity can provide not just to make more effort but to generate the ideas that can move companies forward in far more substantial ways than extra effort ever can.

This chapter provides guidance on how to communicate equity sharing specifically in an LLC as well as strategies to get people more involved.

Explaining How Your Equity Plan Works

Helping employees understand how their equity plans work is not an easy task. Most employees have only a vague and often inaccurate idea

---

1. Douglas L. Kruse, Joseph R. Blasi, and Richard B. Freeman, "Does Linking Worker Pay to Firm Performance Help the Best Firms Do Even Better?," NBER Working Paper No. 17745 (January 2012) (see http://www.nber.org/papers/w17745). The research was done in 2011 and looked at over 300,000 survey respondents in 730 companies that had applied for the "100 Best Companies to Work For in America" list. The list is the creation of the Great Place to Work Institute. The data also include extensive information about company structures and practices.

of how companies make money, what percentage of sales are profits, how stock prices are determined by the market or an appraiser, and how shares get created. Equity awards add another layer of complexity onto that because they are rarely just outright grants of shares but come layered with special rules, and equity awards in LLCs in particular can add yet another layer of complexity because few people understand how an LLC works.

To create a good communications plan, it is important first to understand what makes any kind of communication effective. Several key strategies are critical:

- As many people have reputedly said, it is not what people know that hurts them, it is "what they know that just ain't so." It is essential that companies use surveys and/or focus groups to find out what people know "that just ain't so" so that they can address these issues.

- Divide the communications program into lots of smaller bites delivered regularly. One time, you might explain what a membership interest is; another time, what the tax rules for the awards are. It is easier for people to absorb smaller amounts of information, and the regular provision of communications about the equity awards in itself is a powerful communication that these awards matter.

- Use multiple media—a FAQ on your website, printed materials sent to employee homes, videos, interactive tools to model how an equity award would gain value under various realistic assumptions, small-group meetings, annual all-hands meetings, etc.

- As much as possible, use other employees to explain the plans, not experts. Experts have a hard time remembering what they did not once know and hence assume people understand ideas they do not. Peers don't have that problem and are more credible to other employees as well. To be sure, what they do needs to be vetted by experts, but companies that use peer-based communication find it works very well.

- Provide concrete, specific examples, not just general concepts.

- Don't oversell the plan. Our research shows that employees much prefer honest explanations of potential risks as well as rewards—it shows you are willing to treat them as adults, indeed as fellow owners.

- Use stories. The more that your communication can be based on stories of how the awards have worked for other employees (even if they are in other companies), the more resonant they are. There is a reason newspaper stories on complex topics always start with a story of a specific family or situation—it works.

Given these general principles, you also have to explain plan specifics. People want to know what they will get, when they will get it, what the rules are, and how much they will pay. Use examples to illustrate each point, with scenarios of both rising and falling prices. By focusing just on these issues, doing it often in small bites, and using multiple approaches to explain the same thing, chances are good most employees will get a clear understanding over time. Sadly, however, few companies do much of any of this—they send out a form, a letter from the CEO, and a plan summary, and consider it done. The result is that they spend lots of money on the awards and have lots of confused, uninterested employees.

In an LLC, good communication has to start with explaining how the LLC works. Many people do not know how corporate profits are taxed in general, but, to the extent they do, their model is a C corporation. So companies need to start by explaining that in an LLC, the taxes are passed through to the owners and the board can decide how to allocate the tax obligation (or, if it is done pro-rata in your company, just say that). If your company provides employees with capital interests or profits interests, in general, if they have made a Section 83(b) election and become fully vested, they are treated as a member of the LLC and issued a K-1 statement. This can be an unpleasant and confusing surprise, so make sure that (1) employees fully understand the implications of an 83(b) election and (2) what happens if they get a K-1 statement. Will they receive a distribution of earnings to pay the tax, or is it their responsibility? If the awards are LLC units or unit appreciation rights, this is not an issue.

Second, you need to be very clear about both how awards are issued and why. Lots of companies do the first, but most gloss over the second, just saying it is to reward people. Be very clear about why employees get what they get, what they have to do to earn it, and what you expect from them in return. Perhaps most important, lay out precisely when they will get cashed in. Is it at a sale or IPO only? If so, why? What if employees leave before an event occurs? What if it is uncertain when or even if it will occur? If there is interim liquidity, explain that too. Again, explain in clear, honest terms why you are making these choices.

Finally, explain how they get other questions answered, the procedures for acknowledging the grant, noncompete agreements (if any), when they will get statements, and any other procedural matters. Do not assume people will ask about these or any other issues. Certainly you want to have a Q&A, but often people feel reluctant or embarrassed to ask a question, especially the first one. Instead, try asking people to write down a question before coming to a meeting and then posting FAQs on your internal website.

Sharing Your Numbers Honestly

No matter what decisions your company makes about its equity program design and operation, it is essential to have open and honest communications about how your company is doing. The defining characteristic of the Great Place to Work Institute's "100 Best Companies to Work For in America" is what Robert Levering and Amy Lyman call the "trust index." It measures just how much employees trust management and how much they trust management to trust them.

One of the best ways to build trust is open-book management. Companies using open-book management make a regular practice of keeping employees informed about how the company is doing. Employees feel a lot more like owners when this information is shared. While it is useful to share income statement basics and stock price changes, it is even more useful to share "critical numbers." These are the measures company leaders use to gauge just how they are doing week to week, month to month, and year to year. They are what drives company success, and what leaders worry about if they are not being met. Critical numbers at the corporate level may be profits, but they might also be new customers, new patents, customer service, repeat buyers, overhead absorption, sales growth, and so on. At the operational level, each unit of a company also has critical numbers that measure its contribution.

Sharing these numbers helps employees focus on what matters. It is also very motivating. People will happily play slot machines for hours, even though they usually lose, because there is a game attached. But if they were paid, say, $50 for five hours of pushing the buttons, with no rewards for winning or costs for losing, casinos would go out of business. Business is also a game and is much more fun to play if you know the numbers. Jack Stack, the CEO of SRC, the leading thinker about these issues, says that not keeping employees informed about the score in business is like not telling basketball players who is winning.

In entrepreneurial companies that are looking to be sold or do an IPO, it is especially important to discuss the expected timing of that event, what the company needs to do to prepare for it, what milestones need to be met along the way to reach the company's goals, and what employees can specifically do to help reach them. Too often, company leaders occasionally say that their goal is one of these two events, but employees are left in the dark about management's vision of how to reach them.

Imagine that you are an employee who has just received an equity interest in your company. You've been told the goal is to find another buyer one day so that everyone's equity will be worth a substantial sum. But you have no idea when this might occur, what you can do to make the company more attractive to a potential buyer, or what might happen to your job if you are acquired. All that uncertainty will lead you to view the equity award as a far iffier proposition than it really is. If you do not plan to be sold, then you need to explain what targets the company needs to reach to make it possible to provide interim liquidity (if you have no idea how that will happen, your plan is not really very valuable to anyone).

Your company may also have outside investors. People should know what their roles and expectations are. If there are subsequent investment rounds, explain what this means for the company and the value of the employees' equity interests. As with any other aspect of communicating about equity, you can either explain what is really going on or allow employees to develop their own, usually inaccurate, assumptions.

It is also critical to help employees understand how the company's equity attains value. Very few people understand this process. In most companies, the value of equity is a function of potential future profits. Investors will pay some multiple of expected future earnings to acquire the company. How much they pay depends on the rate of return they expect, which in turn is driven by what else they could do with the money and how much risk your projected future earnings entail.

One way we at the NCEO explain this to employees is our "Harry the Horse" game. We divide employees into groups of six to eight people. Half are sellers and half are buyers of Harry, a three-year-old racehorse that, after all costs, made $50,000 in profit last year and may be able to race for several more years. The buyers come up with a price they would offer and the sellers a price they would sell for, and then they negotiate. Each group reports back its results (some groups never find common ground) and the factors that led to them. The leader adds other factors that come into play that were not raised. Factors should include Harry-specific risks, industry risks, economy risks, returns on investments of varying risk, how tied up the money will be for how long, and Harry's long-term asset value (stud fees if he races well, glue if not). Then explain that investors look at all these things, estimate the combination of the present value of Harry's future earnings and asset value, and decide, given the risk of buying Harry versus other investments (stocks, bonds, buying stock in one company, etc.) what rate of return they need. If they want a 25% return, then they would pay four times earnings, including stud fees or the going rate of glue.

The point of the game is not to educate people about horse racing, but to show that a potential investor would look at your company in much the same way. The key takeaway is that for each additional dollar of profit the company makes, the stock price (or, in this case, the member interest price) increases not by one dollar but by some multiple, such as four in the above example. That helps people understand why ownership can be uniquely valuable if you make profits or can convince investors one day you will.

Note that there are some technology companies where profits matter much less. Their model may be that if they develop a significant new technology, even one they cannot make money on, another company may buy them because it believes that it can make a profit on it. If that is your business model, then the critical numbers you need to focus on relate to progress toward the development of that product or products.

Creating an Ownership Culture

The common notion is that if employees are granted significant equity stakes in their companies, they will be motivated to think and act like owners. To some extent, this can happen. The image of the 20-something software engineer spending 80-plus hours a week and sleeping on the floor under his desk while working all weekend to get a program out is not just apocryphal. But motivation at work turns out to be a lot more complex than rational calculations about money. The best-selling author Daniel Pink, for instance, says the keys to motivating people at work are purpose, autonomy, and challenge. Financial rewards do matter, he says, if only because absent them people feel manipulated. But when motivation is based solely on money, work can become a chore, not a passion. Moreover, when the reward shrinks or disappears, even for a time, people can become severely demotivated.

As I was writing this, for instance, I saw a story about an employee at Zynga. After it went public in 2011, its share price tanked. Some insiders had been able to get out and make vast sums of money, but employees were subject to lock-ups before selling their restricted stock shares and ended up with awards worth little or nothing. One employee was quoted as saying that he worked 100 hours a week for three years before the IPO in anticipation of a huge payoff even though he felt his managers treated him badly and he didn't really like the job. That story might have been very different if he felt that his work was intrinsically rewarding, that he was treated well by managers, and that his job had a larger purpose. Indeed, companies like Google and Southwest Airlines, both of which use broad-based equity awards, have maintained high employee motivation even during sharp slumps in share prices, because either cultures are so strong and people feel much more like owners in terms of how the company treats them day to day.

So what makes for this kind of ownership culture? The research on this point, including the huge project with the 100 Best Companies to Work For in America list referred to earlier, is very clear. The best companies not only use open-book management but also create specific structures for employees to share ideas and information. These commonly include work teams, ad hoc groups, devolution of decision-making authority to lower-level employees, company-wide staff meetings to discuss ideas and strategy, web-based systems for collaboration and idea sharing, and other approaches to make employee involvement not just something that is allowed (as in open-door policies) but an expected part of the job.

Conclusion

It doesn't make sense to give away significant equity in your company and then not make a sustained effort to make sure people know how it works, how the company makes money and grows, and how ownership interests attain value. But the real communications are not just what you say but what you do. Companies that communicate ownership by sharing their performance numbers and creating structured opportunities (and expectations) that employees will contribute ideas and information to move the company forward can—and, the research shows, does—significantly outperform their more conventional peers.

Chapter 8

Drafting Considerations for LLC Equity Compensation Plans

Amy Pocino Kelly, Erin Randolph-Williams, and Samuel P. Bryant

Limited liability companies (LLCs) have become a popular organizational form for many privately held businesses, as they provide attractive flexibility in structuring the rights and obligations of their owners, commonly referred to as members. LLCs are eligible to be treated as partnerships for tax purposes, which permits LLCs to offer additional compensation structures not available to entities taxed as corporations. This chapter generally discusses matters to be considered when drafting the plan documents and award agreements governing equity compensation in LLCs treated as partnerships for tax purposes. However, this discussion is intended only as a high-level primer on the topic and does not consider all possible issues that may be relevant in a particular situation. LLCs, their principals, and their service providers should seek specific legal advice before implementing or participating in a particular form of equity compensation plan.

The most common forms of equity compensation in an LLC (classified as a partnership for tax purposes) consist of capital interests, profits interests, and options. Many companies, however, will choose to use a synthetic version of these awards (sometimes called phantom awards) that give employees the right to a stated value but not actual equity. Each form of equity compensation has its own set of benefits and tradeoffs that must be considered before granting to a particular service provider.

Often, an LLC will wish to establish a broad, omnibus plan in order to permit the grant of awards of each type, as circumstances may warrant. The plan sets the overall rules, but a separate grant agreement with the recipient will spell out the specific rules for that recipient. These do not have to be the same for each participant unless the plan requires that.

Structure of Plan Documentation

The terms and conditions of equity awards that may be granted to service providers may be set forth directly in the LLC's primary governing operating agreement. However, because such provisions are generally relevant only to grantees, not to the ordinary equity owners of the LLC, often the LLC will choose to establish a separate equity plan document, under authority granted in the LLC's operating agreement, to govern awards to service providers. This chapter generally assumes that a separate plan document will be adopted. The plan should provide that it is a condition precedent to the receipt of equity under the plan that a grantee execute a joinder agreement to the LLC's operating agreement, as in effect from time to time.

Administration of the Plan

As noted above, the plan should be adopted and approved in accordance with the relevant requirements under the LLC's operating agreement. The plan should then set forth the terms under which it will be administered, including:

- Whether the plan will be administered directly by the governing person or body (such as a managing member or board of managers) of the LLC, or by a committee appointed for the purpose (such as a compensation committee of the board). The plan should also indicate whether such committee may delegate its authority to a subcommittee or plan administrator, in whole or in part. (In this chapter, we refer generally to the "administrator" as the person or body granted general authority under the plan document.)
- The actions the administrator of the plan is authorized to take, including determining grantees, types and terms, amending awards, and resolving other matters that may arise under the plan.

- The discretion the administrator of the plan may use in administering the plan. Generally, LLCs will wish to vest in the administrator the sole discretion to administer and interpret the plan, make factual determinations, and adopt rules to govern the plan, and the plan will provide that such actions are conclusive and binding on all parties.

Forms of Awards

As noted above, the plan may provide for the grant of options (non-qualified options) and awards of equity representing capital interests and profits interests in the LLC. It is also possible for the plan to specify synthetic equity forms of these awards (what we call unit right and unit right appreciation plans in this book). In the sections below, we discuss general considerations and drafting concerns raised by each type of award.

Equity Issuance Limitations

It is advisable that the plan authorize a maximum amount of equity that may be issued under the plan, whether in the form of grants of capital or profits interests or of equity issued upon the exercise of options. This authorization may be in the form of an aggregate limit or a limit for each form of award. This provision of the plan should be carefully coordinated with the provisions of the LLC's operating agreement describing the equity interests issuable by the LLC. If the LLC's equity is not unitized but is rather referenced in the form of percentage interests, an LLC should consider whether to unitize the equity so that a certain number of units are authorized. Although not required, when implementing an equity compensation plan in an LLC, many LLCs choose to unitize as it is simpler for many grantees to understand their stake in the LLC in terms of units rather than percentages of ownership that will change as members of the LLC change. For purposes of these drafting considerations, we will assume that the LLC has been unitized.

In the event of a capital event affecting the number of units authorized, the plan should include a provision that provides that the maximum number of units may be adjusted from time to time in accordance with the plan's and the operating agreement's applicable amendment terms. The plan may also set forth the conditions under which the number of authorized units will be adjusted (such as in the event of a spinoff, unit split, or other capitalization change), and any limitations on the administrator's authority to determine that such an adjustment is appropriate.

Eligibility

The plan should describe the persons eligible to receive awards, including employees and other service providers, such as director and advisors and consultants performing services for the LLC and its subsidiaries. As discussed in more detail below, in order to qualify for certain exceptions to registering an LLC's equity with the Securities and Exchange Commission (SEC), grantees should be limited to employees and only certain service providers who are not employees.

Compliance Note: Partner-Employee Status

A grantee who receives a unit (capital or profits interest) award, or exercises an option and acquires units, will become a member of the LLC and will subsequently be taxed as a member. The IRS takes the position that a member of an LLC cannot also be an employee of the LLC. Instead, once an employee owns an equity interest in an LLC, the individual is treated as a partner, and, as a result:

- the member should receive only a Schedule K-1, and not a Form W-2;
- the member's salary will likely be treated as a partnership "guaranteed payment";
- the LLC should not withhold income taxes or make employment tax payments attributable to member payments;
- the member must pay estimated taxes quarterly;
- the member cannot participate in certain tax-advantaged benefit plans;
- the member must pay self-employment taxes on its share of LLC income as self-employment income; and

- the member likely will be required to file tax returns in all jurisdictions in which the LLC files tax returns.

This means that an LLC member will be subject to self-employment taxes on its share of income generated by the LLC's activities. The tax partner status of the grantee also limits the grantee's tax advantages with respect to employee benefits, health insurance, and other fringe benefits. For example, being a partner affects the grantee's ability to exclude from income the health insurance premiums paid by the LLC on the grantee's behalf. As a member, the grantee also cannot participate in "cafeteria plans" (a reimbursement plan governed by Section 125 of the Internal Revenue Code of 1986, as amended (the "Code"), which allows employees to contribute a certain amount of their gross income to designated accounts before taxes are calculated).

In general, once a member of an LLC, the member's tax filings and other compliance responsibilities may become more complicated and costly, which should be considered seriously by both the LLC and the potential member before an LLC grants a capital interest or profits interest to an employee. Many employees, particularly those who are not in senior management, do not want to be subjected to the additional complexities that come along with being a member of an LLC. For these reasons, options, which can be structured to allow the employee and the employer to control the timing of whether and when the employee becomes a member of an LLC, may be preferable, albeit at the "cost" of not being able to treat any portion of their income or gain in an exit or liquidity event as capital gains.

Under certain alternative organizational structures, recipients of LLC interests may remain W-2 employees of a subsidiary C corporation of the LLC, but that is beyond the scope of this discussion and is discussed in more detail in chapter 4.

Options

As with options granted by corporations, an option granted by an LLC entitles the grantee to purchase, at a specified exercise price, a number of units of the LLC at some time in the future, subject to the option's vesting and other terms and conditions. Options granted by an LLC will be "nonqualified options." "Incentive stock options" within the meaning of Section 422 of the Code may not be granted by an LLC because the Code requires that incentive stock options may only be granted by corporations to employees of a corporation.

Options are often preferred by service providers because they allow the service provider to control when the tax event will occur. As discussed in detail in chapter 3, in general, there is no taxable event on the date of grant of an option. When the grantee exercises an option, the grantee will recognize ordinary income in an amount equal to the excess of the fair market value of the purchased interests at the time of exercise over the exercise price.

An option holder is generally not an equity holder for federal tax law purposes with respect to the underlying LLC interest until the date of exercise. In most cases, the grantee does not exercise the option until an exit or liquidity event. Often, option grantees are rank-and-file employees who do not want the complications of being a partner in a tax partnership described below, and also want to avoid a "phantom income" event (i.e., a tax recognition event that does not produce liquid proceeds from which to pay the tax) that would result from the exercise of the option. To avoid these issues, option holders accept that they will participate in the sale event at ordinary income rates rather than at capital gains rates.

Fair Market Value

As discussed in detail in chapter 3, the exercise price of nonqualified options must be equal to or greater than the fair market value of a unit on the date of grant in order to be exempt from Section 409A of the Code. For the reasons discussed in chapter 3, it is usually preferable for the options to be exempt from Section 409A of the Code, and accordingly, the plan should require that the exercise price be not less than the fair market value of a unit on the date of grant, and it should specify the method(s) by which the LLC will determine the fair market value of units.

Vesting and Exercisability

The schedule by which options become vested and exercisable (e.g., 25% each anniversary of the grant date for four years, cliff vesting at 100%

after two years, or vesting upon the achievement of specific financial performance goals) may be set forth in the plan, but, more commonly, LLCs will reserve the determination of vesting terms for individual award agreements.

Generally, options may be exercised at any time after they become vested. However, in order to ease the burden and costs associated with the booking up of capital accounts that will occur on exercise, LLCs may wish to limit the exercise of options to specific dates, e.g., December 31 of each year.

If desired, the plan may permit the LLC to grant options with terms that permit the early exercise of an option (before vesting) and receipt of restricted capital units that will vest over the same schedule as was applicable under the terms of the option.

The plan should include a provision in order to comply with the Fair Labor Standards Act requirement that options granted to nonexempt employees should not be exercisable for a period of at least six months from the date of grant (except in the event of the employee's death, disability, or retirement, a change of control, or other circumstances permitted by regulations).

The plan should describe the method by which options may be exercised. Typically, the option price may be paid in cash, by delivering units already owned by the grantee, or by any other method permitted by the administrator.

Impact of Termination of Service

The plan or individual award agreement should specify how options are treated in the event of a termination of employment or service. Generally, LLCs provide that any portion of the option that is not forfeited (generally because it has already become vested or becomes vested in connection with the transaction) may be exercised within a specified time after termination. A common approach is to provide that options may be exercised for 90 days after termination of employment or service, or up to one year in the event of a termination as a result of death or disability.

If the grantee's employment is terminated for "cause," companies generally provide in the plan or individual award agreement that all options will be forfeited and may not be exercised. The plan may contain its own definition of "cause," refer to another shared agreement (such as the LLC operating agreement), or provide a default definition that may be overridden if the grantee has a definition in, for example, an employment agreement.

Additionally, the LLC may wish to provide that if the administrator determines that the grantee has engaged in conduct that constitutes "cause" at any time, including after termination for another reason, the options will terminate.

The regulations issued under Section 409A provide that an amendment to a previously granted option to provide a grantee with an additional period beyond the time originally prescribed in the option grant is permissible as long as such extension does not extend beyond the earlier of (1) the original maximum term of the option or (2) 10 years from the original grant date. If an option is extended beyond the maximum permissible period and the option is "in the money" (i.e., the exercise price is less than the current fair market value of the underlying units on the date of the extension), then the extension will be treated as an additional deferral feature. This means that the option will be subject to Section 409A from the original date of grant, and generally will fail to meet such requirements. Failure to comply with the requirements of Section 409A will result in significant adverse tax consequences to the grantee, as discussed in chapter 3.

Unit Awards

In addition to options, the LLC may grant awards of units directly in the form of either "capital interests" or "profits interests." Awards of units, whether capital or profits interests, may be immediately fully vested at grant, or may be made subject to restrictions that lapse over a period of time or according to other criteria (such as the achievement of performance goals). As noted above, the LLC's operating agreement's provisions regarding issuable equity interests will need to be coordinated with the awards covered by the plans, such as to provide expressly for the grant of profits interests. Once a grantee receives either capital units or profits interests, the grantee will become a member of the LLC. Unless otherwise desired, the plan should provide that grantees will have the right to vote and receive distributions paid on such units, including during a restricted period.

A "capital interest" generally entitles the grantee to an immediate economic interest in the underlying assets of the LLC (i.e., the share in the proceeds if, at the time of grant, the LLC sells all of its assets at fair market value and distributes the proceeds in complete liquidation), as well as the ability to share in future profits of the LLC.

If an interest in the LLC is not entitled to a distribution under this approach, it may potentially be classified as a "profits interest" for tax purposes. A profits interest entitles the grantee to share in the future earnings and appreciation in the value of the LLC arising after the date of grant. In some cases, while options are effectively economic equivalent to a profits interest, a profits interest grantee may be eligible for more favorable tax treatment. Because option grantees typically do not exercise their options until an exit or liquidity event, option proceeds are generally taxed as compensation at ordinary income rates. A profits interest grantee may be able to receive exit or liquidity event proceeds taxed at preferential capital gains rate. However, some LLCs and grantees may nevertheless prefer option grants, because the profits interest grantee, as an LLC member, is subject to additional tax and administrative complexities, as described above.

Vesting

As with options, the schedule by which units become vested (if they are not fully vested on grant) may be set forth in the plan or in individual award agreements. In general, the term "vested" with respect to unit awards is intended to refer to units for which a "substantial risk of forfeiture" has expired with respect to such units within the meaning of Section 83 of the Code and the regulations thereunder. As noted above, grantees of "unvested" units under the plan are intended to be treated as the owners of such units for legal purposes and tax purposes upon grant irrespective of the fact that they may be required to surrender these units back to the LLC in the event the applicable vesting conditions are not met, or a forfeiture condition (such as termination for cause) occurs.

Impact of Termination of Service

The plan or individual award agreement should specify how units granted as capital interests or profits interests are treated in the event of a termination of employment or service. In most circumstances, the unvested portion of the award is forfeited upon termination of employment or service, and the vested portion may be subject to the LLC's right to repurchase the vested units for the then-current fair market value, or even forfeited if the termination is for cause.

Withholding

The plan should provide that grants will be subject to withholding of applicable income tax, employment tax, applicable federal, state, local or foreign income tax, employment or payroll tax, Social Security tax, or other amounts required to be withheld, collected, or accounted for by the LLC in connection with any taxable event with respect to the grant.

Transfers and Sales

The plan should specify any limitations on grantees' ability to transfer awards made under the plan. Generally, companies will wish to provide that a grantee may not sell, assign, transfer, pledge, or otherwise dispose of options (at any time) or units (at any time during which any restricted period applies), except in connection with estate planning, valid domestic relations orders, or as otherwise permitted by the administrator. Any permitted recipient should be required, like the original grantee, to subscribe to and be bound by the terms of the operating agreement or other governing document applicable to unitholders.

If the plan permits the transfer of options after any restrictions lapse, the plan should also address any right of first refusal or similar right of the LLC. Often, companies will wish to reserve the right of the LLC, if a unitholder desires to sell to a third party, to instead purchase the units itself, following a notice of the terms of the proposed sale by the unitholder. In addition, the LLC may wish to reserve a right to repurchase units at any time following a grantee's termination of employment or service, at a price specified in the plan. Generally, such rights will lapse by their terms in the event of an initial public offering of the LLC.

Change of Control Provisions

The plan should address the impact of a "change of control" (or liquidity event) transaction. Such transaction events may be defined in the plan or defined by reference to provisions of the LLC operating agreement, in order to coordinate the provision with terms governing the interests of other unitholders.

Often, rather than prescribing specific consequences, companies will provide in a plan that, upon a change of control, the administrator will have the discretion to determine whether outstanding options will become fully exercisable and unit awards will become fully vested, and/or how (if at all) outstanding awards will be terminated, replaced, assumed, or settled in cash or other property. However, the LLC may provide for more specific terms (such as automatic accelerated vesting upon a change of control or a termination in connection with such an event) in individual grant agreements.

Unit Rights and Unit Appreciation Plans

As discussed in chapter 3, many companies may not wish to issue actual equity awards, whether options, profits interests, or capital interests. This is especially true if the ability for employees to have their awards taxed under capital gains rules is not a significant factor, as would normally be the case for all but highly compensated employees.

Unit rights plans give employees the right to the value of a stated number of LLC units, while unit appreciation plans give them the right to the increase in the value. The drafting considerations for these plans can follow those for the other plans listed above for issues such as termination, vesting, exercisability, eligibility, and change of control, but note that the employee will not be considered an owner and will not get a K-1 statement and the awards are not subject to securities law issues.

To avoid any potential tax issues, appreciation awards should be granted with a base price at fair market value. In any event, the awards should be designed to comply with, or be exempt from, Section 409A of the Code.

Compliance Note: Federal and State Securities Laws

The application of federal and state securities laws to the sale or grant of units under the plan should be considered. Typically, when a company issues securities, the securities must be registered with the SEC unless the transaction qualifies for an exemption from registration. An exemption from the registration requirement means that companies do not need to make SEC filings or pay any federal filing fees.

Most commonly, LLCs use Rule 701 under the Securities Act of 1933, as amended, to grant equity compensation to its service providers without registering the equity with the SEC. Rule 701 allows private companies to offer their securities as part of a written compensation plan to employees, members of the board of directors, and certain consultants without having to register their units under the federal securities laws. Companies hoping to take advantage of Rule 701 need to satisfy several additional conditions:

1. The issuer cannot offer the securities to raise capital;
2. The aggregate sales (not offerings) of stocks sold in reliance upon Rule 701 during any consecutive 12-month period must not exceed the greater of (a) $1,000,000; (b) 15% of the total assets of the issuer (or of the issuer's parent company if the issuer is a wholly owned subsidiary); or (c) 15% of the outstanding amount of the class of securities being offered and sold;
3. The issuer must deliver to investors a copy of a compensatory benefit plan or a contract; and
4. For sales over $10 million during any consecutive 12-month period, the issuer must provide relevant disclosures to investors, including a summary of the material terms of the plan, information about the risks associated with the investment, and financial statements.

Additionally, there are special requirements for consultants and advisors purchasing or being granted securities. In order to qualify for the exemption under Rule 701, offers and sales to consultants and advisors must be made for compensatory purposes only, not for other purposes, such as capital-raising transactions or promotion of the issuer's securities. The consultants and advisors must be natural persons providing bona fide services at the time of the offer.

In measuring sales, all options granted during the period are considered part of the aggregate sales, with the option price defined as of the date of grant. For grants of units in exchange for services, the fair market value of the securities is taken into account.

A company must monitor its equity grants to ensure that, in any consecutive 12-month period, the grants do not exceed the foregoing limitations, or that another securities law exemption is available. If a Rule 701 exemption is not available, there are other exemptions an LLC can consider, such as under the accredited investor exceptions under Regulation D of the Securities Act. If another exemption, such as the accredited investor exception, is relied upon, the documentation used for individual grants may need to be updated to include appropriate representations regarding the eligibility of grantees for such treatment.

In addition, even if a federal registration exemption is available, companies are still required to comply with state securities laws, and anti-fraud, civil liability, or other provisions of federal securities laws. Issuing companies should not equate the exemption from SEC registration with an exemption from other relevant regulations. Among other requirements, the company may be required to make filings with the securities commissions of the states in which the recipients live (and often pay filing fees) to perfect the exemption. Many states have exemptions similar to Rule 701 or require an offering to meet the requirements of Rule 701. However, careful attention should be paid to the local requirements in each state in which grantees live.

Rights of Grantees

The plan should provide that the plan does not entitle any employee, service provider or any other person to any right to a grant under the plan, or any rights to continued employment.

Funding of the Plan

The plan should provide that it is unfunded and that the LLC is not required to establish any fund for payment of any grants.

Compliance with Law

The plan should include a general compliance-with-law provision, including a provision that awards are intended to comply with or be exempt from Section 409A, and to comply with applicable securities laws. The provision should permit the administrator to revoke any grant if it is contrary to law or modify a grant or the plan to bring it into compliance with applicable law. The plan should also provide that each grantee is solely responsible for the tax consequences of grants under the plan, and the LLC will not have any responsibility or liability if a grant does not meet any applicable requirements of Section 409A or another law.

Non-U.S. Grants

If grants are made under the plan to persons living outside the United States, it may be appropriate to add special provisions to comply with local law. The plan may also include a general authorization to create sub-plans drafted to comply with local requirements as the relevant jurisdictions may not be known at the time the plan is established.

About the Authors

Casey S. August is a partner at Morgan Lewis. His practice focuses on U.S. federal tax planning and implementation matters. Representing clients across industries, he advises on structuring and documentation issues for mergers and acquisitions, energy project financings, joint venture collaborations, and intellectual property transfers. Casey also counsels clients on issues involving choice of entity and cross-border structuring and planning, as well as on IRS private letter ruling submissions and securities filings.

Samuel P. Bryant is an associate at Morgan Lewis. He advises clients on a wide range of issues related to executive compensation, employee benefits, and pension plan fiduciary matters. He represents public and private companies in the design, negotiation, and implementation of incentive compensation plans, employment agreements and separation arrangements, including in the context of complex corporate transactions. Sam also advises clients on ERISA fiduciary duties, prohibited transaction rules, and related regulatory issues impacting pension plan sponsors, fiduciaries, service providers, and counterparties.

Amy Pocino Kelly is a partner at Morgan Lewis. She is the deputy practice leader for the employee benefits and executive compensation practice. Amy's practice focuses on providing strategic, day-to-day guidance on employee benefit plan matters to plan sponsors, including public and private companies, tax-exempt organizations, and governmental employers. She counsels these clients on the design, governance, operation, and compliance of qualified and nonqualified retirement plans, equity and executive compensation arrangements, and welfare benefit plans. Amy also represents plan sponsors in audit and correction matters before the U.S. Department of Labor (DOL) and the Internal Revenue Service (IRS).

Wells Miller is counsel at Choate Hall & Stewart LLP. Mr. Miller focuses on executive compensation issues, particularly in the context of mergers and acquisitions. Mr. Miller assists the firm's clients in drafting and maintaining nonqualified deferred compensation plans, equity and equity-based incentive compensation arrangements (including compensatory partnership interests), severance plans, transaction bonus plans, and executive employment agreements. He also advises clients on matters related to ERISA, with a particular focus on issues related to private equity funds and lenders. Mr. Miller received his BA in politics, philosophy, and economics from Pomona College and his JD from Boston University, where he served as editor-in-chief of the American Journal of Law & Medicine.

Alan A. Nadel is the managing director of Strategic Apex Group LLC, a compensation consulting firm with offices in New York, Los Angeles, and Denver. He has more than 45 years of experience serving a diverse range of clients, advising on matters relating to governance, executive and board of directors compensation, employee benefits, retirement programs, ESOPs, and income and estate planning. In his current practice, Alan advises executives and boards of directors about the design and implementation of executive and director programs, including strategic, financial, funding, accounting, and tax considerations. He also has represented various companies and senior executives in negotiations concerning employment agreements, severance programs, and change-in-control arrangements. Alan has provided expert testimony in both civil and criminal matters. Clients include public and private companies, domestic as well as international. Before establishing his consulting firm, Alan was a partner in a major accounting firm, where he established the compensation consulting practice and served as managing partner for human capital. Alan started his career with the Internal Revenue Service. He coauthored the first and second editions of *Accounting for Equity Compensation* and *Equity Compensation for Limited Liability Companies,* and he is a contributing author for *Employee*

Benefits in Mergers & Acquisitions, The Employee Benefits Handbook, Compensation Committee Handbook, the first through fourth editions of *The Stock Options Book,* and the first and second editions of *Executive Compensation in ESOP Companies.* Alan has lectured at various law schools and business schools and is a frequent speaker before professional and industry groups.

Erin Randolph-Williams is of counsel at Morgan Lewis. She is part of a team that helps clients find solutions to their employee benefits–related problems. She counsels clients on employee benefits matters, including design, implementation, and administration of cash or deferred compensation arrangements, nonqualified deferred compensation plans, and executive and equity compensation arrangements. Erin negotiates employment agreements and severance arrangements for senior executives, and advises clients on all employee benefits and compensation-related aspects of mergers, acquisitions, sales, and spin-offs.

Corey Rosen is the founder and former executive director of the National Center for Employee Ownership (NCEO) and now is its senior staff member. Corey has spoken on various subjects related to employee ownership all over the world with government, business, and union leaders, and he is regularly quoted in leading magazines and newspapers. He has appeared on national television and radio programs and also has authored four books on employee ownership, plus more than 100 articles for various business, academic, and professional publications. He has authored or coauthored several of the NCEO's practical and research publications.

About the NCEO

The National Center for Employee Ownership (NCEO) is widely considered to be the leading authority on employee ownership in the U.S. and the world. Established in 1981 as a nonprofit information and membership organization, it now has more than 3,000 members. It is funded almost entirely through the work it does.

The NCEO's mission is to provide practical resources and objective, reliable information about employee ownership to businesses, employees, and the public. As part of the NCEO's commitment to providing objective information, it does not lobby or provide ongoing consulting services. The NCEO publishes a variety of materials on employee ownership and participation; holds dozens of seminars, webinars, and conferences on employee ownership annually; and offers online courses. The NCEO's work also includes extensive contacts with the media, both through articles written for trade and professional publications and through interviews with reporters.

Membership Benefits

NCEO members receive the following benefits and more:

- The members-only newsletter *Employee Ownership Report.*
- Access to the NCEO's members-only website resources, including the Document Library, ESOP Q&A, and more.
- Free access to both live and recorded webinars.
- Discounts on books and other NCEO products and services.
- The right to contact the NCEO for answers to questions.

To join or order publications, visit our website at www.nceo.org or telephone us at 510-208-1300.

Made in the USA
Coppell, TX
13 March 2023

14204553R00068